SHAOLIN LOHAN KUNG-FU

少林國術隨身寶典

達摩祖師

Painting of Ta Mo, by Pye Ling Shan Rur; calligraphy by Shi
Mit Tu. Courtesy, Penang Shaolin Athletic Association.

SHAOLIN
Lohan
Kung-Fu

by P'ng Chye Khim
and Donn F. Draeger

CHARLES E. TUTTLE COMPANY
Rutland · Vermont : Tokyo · Japan

Published by the Charles E. Tuttle Company, Inc.
of Rutland, Vermont & Tokyo, Japan
with editorial offices at
1-2-6 Suido, Bunkyo-ku, Tokyo 112

LCC Card No. 78-62671
ISBN 0-8048-1698-0

First edition, 1979
First paperback edition, 1991
Fifth printing, 1997

Printed in Singapore

Table of Contents

Preface

THIS IS an introductory book on the subject of *shaolin*. Shaolin is a popular form of Chinese hand-to-hand art that originated centuries ago and that continues to be an important part of the lives of many millions of Chinese and an unknown number of non-Chinese peoples throughout the world.

The system of shaolin that is the basis of this book is that of the Hood Khar *pai*, a Chinese organization founded by a Shaolin Temple monk, Sik Koe Chum. In 1940, Sik Koe Chum left South China for Medan, Indonesia. He moved to Singapore in 1947; then, in 1955, he made his way to Penang, Malaysia, to repair a temple there. In 1956, he founded the Hood Khar pai in Penang and, until his death in 1960, dedicated himself totally to the dissemination of genuine shaolin teachings. This book is dedicated to his memory.

The shaolin of the Hood Khar pai is not necessarily the best of the possibly many thousands of different shaolin systems in existence, but we have chosen Hood Khar pai shaolin because it truly represents the use of a genuine, traditional Chinese hand-to-hand art in a new role beneficial to modern society.

All Chinese hand-to-hand arts have both good and bad points; no system is any better than the trainees who practice it. It does not matter which art is the best. What matters is whether the student is satisfied that that in which he engages is good for him and will mold him into a wholesome person prepared for his role in an ever-changing and always difficult world. Each trainee must be motivated to study diligently the art of his choice.

There will be those who will criticize us for breaking the orthodox veil of secrecy that surrounds all genuine shaolin teachings. However, we believe that this narrow interpretation of orthodoxy has already caused too much of what constitutes shaolin art to perish and be forever lost to modern man. This loss is a shameful and needless waste of an important part of Chinese culture. This book is a small attempt to forestall any future loss of the shaolin art. We hope this book will serve as a record of some of the important aspects of shaolin and will stimulate others to write about shaolin. To those who say that the contents of this book do not represent the pure art of shaolin, we address the following: The present form of the airplane is not an example of its prototype or pure form, but there are few people who can validly argue that the new airplane is less efficient or less useful than the old. Likewise, improved records and feats of physical prowess in all kinds of sport clearly indicate that the modern entities are in no way inferior to their ancestral forms.

The system of romanization used here for Chinese words and names follows that of the International Hoplological Research Center, Hawaii, as adapted from the Hood Khar pai and the Chinese Post Office system.

P'NG CHYE KHIM
DONN F. DRAEGER

Penang, Malaysia

Acknowledgments

MANY PEOPLE were responsible for making this book possible, some more directly than others. We extend our gratitude to all who contributed so generously of their time and experience while this book was being prepared. Special thanks go to Yuk Yin, priest of the Song Kheng See in Penang and patron of the Hood Khar pai; to Chew Ah Pee and Lee Ah Choo, who served as the models, together with the Chinese coauthor, for many of the illustrations of training exercises and techniques; to Khoo Kay Chee, who translated the technical portions of the text; to Pye Ling Shan Rur, who painted the likeness of Ta Mo, and to Shi Mit Tu, who was the calligrapher for the painting; to D'Arcy Champney, whose skillful artwork heightens the explanations of fundamentals and techniques; to Kobayashi Ichiro and the members of his photographic staff for the special care taken in preparing the photographic illustrations; and to Gail Brooks, who typed the final manuscript.

少林

1

Background of Shaolin

Legend

Oral tradition tells us that about A.D. 520 an Indian Buddhist monk arrived in China. He eventually settled at the Shaolin Temple at Sung Shan in Honan province. This monk was P'u-t'i-ta-mo, or Ta Mo (Bohdidharma), as he is more popularly known. It is said that the original Shaolin Temple (*Shaolin-ssu*) was located just below the peak and on the northern side of Sung Shan, one of the great mountains in Honan. This temple was allegedly built by Emperor Hsiao Wen of the Northern Wei dynasty (A.D. 386–534).

Ta Mo introduced some very conservative Buddhist doctrines at the Honan Shaolin Temple, as he was opposed to the highly ritualistic and extravagantly ceremonial religious practices that he found there. He held that the practice of sitting in solitude for the purpose of meditating was the core of a superior kind of religious Buddhism, and in support of his belief he allegedly sat in meditation for nine years while facing a wall in the courtyard of that temple. Ta Mo's kind of Buddhism is said to be the basis of what is today known as Ch'an, and he is considered its First Patriarch.

At the Shaolin Temple in Honan, Ta Mo became disturbed over the fact that monks there frequently fell asleep during meditation. He thereupon designed special exercises by which the monks could increase their stamina and so stay their weariness. In the *I-Chin Ching* (Muscle-Change Classic), a work that is attributed to Ta Mo, we find described and illustrated eighteen such basic exercises for the purpose of improving one's general health. These exercises are believed by some people to be the basis of *shaolin,* a category of hand-to-hand arts, so named after the temple at which Ta Mo meditated.

Thereafter, the Honan Shaolin Temple attracted men from all walks of life, and became a source of and training ground for persons who engaged in the practice of fighting arts. Many of the exponents of fighting arts who trained at the Honan Shaolin Temple became involved in the political intrigues of the various Chinese dynasties that were constantly seeking to become the absolute ruler of China. For example, during the T'ang dynasty (A.D. 618–907), heroic fighting monks such as Chin Ts'ao, Hui Yang, and T'an Tsung of the Honan Shaolin Temple were instrumental in the T'ang defeat of the rebel Wang Shih-ch'ing.

A second Shaolin Temple, supposedly constructed over a thousand years ago at Chuan Chow in Fukien province in South China, is also recorded in Chinese legends. A Buddhist priest named Ta Tsun-shen is believed to have founded it. This temple, too, eventually became a center for combative activity, and consequently is said to have played an important role in the political histories of various dynasties.

Both temples, the one at Sung Shan in the north and that at Chuan Chow in the south, were, during years of warring, frequently razed on the grounds of alleged sedition against the government. Only a few of the occupants of these temples managed to escape the wrath of the imperial troops sent to destroy them. The more fortunate of these fugitives avoided detection by going their separate ways to other areas of China and elsewhere, where they continued their study and practice of fighting arts.

The fame of the Fukien Shaolin Temple became particularly widespread as exponents of combative arts converged there to further their skills. The Ch'ing (Manchu) government (1644–1911) was grateful to this temple when, during the reign of Emperor K'ang Hsi (1672), 108 Shaolin Temple monks volunteered for military service against the marauding bands of barbarians who were massing on China's western borders. These monks displayed skill and heroism in expelling the invaders. But a short time later, when it was discovered that the Fukien Shaolin Temple monks were actually rebels who dreamed of restoring the Ming government and who were searching for an opportunity to launch their own uprising, the Ch'ing ordered the destruction of the Fukien Shaolin Temple and the massacre of its occupants. Five monks, later honored as the Five Early Founding Fathers, escaped by hiding under a bridge, and were taken into hiding by five brave men who were subsequently referred to as the Five Middle Founding Fathers. In turn, these ten rebels were joined by five other monks, the Five Later Founding Fathers, and together with the priest Wan Yun-loong (Ten-Thousand-Cloud Dragon) and Ch'en Chin-nan (Great Ancestor), did battle against the Manchu forces in the northern province of Hopei. The spirit of their uprising spread rapidly southward and inspired others to join in the fight against the Manchu government. Each of the five original monk fugitives from the Fukien Shaolin Temple is believed to have established his own particular kind of shaolin, and collectively these five kinds of shaolin are traditionally held to be the prototypes of shaolin as we know it today.

History

Most of what is traditionally said about the Shaolin Temples is unconfirmed and unverifiable; it is the basis of endless variations on colorful but highly improbable happenings such as form the bulk of plots of Chinese folklore and the dramatized versions of heroics that take place on the modern Chinese popular stage. But, because there may be some factual basis for even the most exaggerated of these stories, modern exponents and scholars of Chinese hand-to-hand arts continue their efforts to discover the truth about the Shaolin Temples and their effect on Chinese society.

The traditional date of Ta Mo's arrival in China (*c*. A.D. 520) is suspect; recent investigations made by historians indicate that he may have come to China as early as A.D. 420–79. We know little beyond the facts that he actually lived and that he came to China. There are no historical records of his existence in India. Further, there is no proof of his authorship of the Muscle-Change Classic (*I-Chin Ching*). Nor are the eighteen basic exercises in that book directly related to Chinese combative arts, being more concerned with calisthenics performed from static stances and postures and designed to strengthen the body and mind so that the performer will be more receptive to meditative discipline. It is now known that combative arts of a shaolin-like nature existed long before Ta Mo came to China, and that at least some of these arts were initially practiced in places other than the Shaolin Temples. Scholars, therefore, generally agree that Ta Mo did not introduce shaolin methods to China.

During the centuries that followed Ta Mo's death, both clergy and lay persons who were advocates of Taoism, Ch'an, and other forms of Buddhism contributed much to the development and systematization of shaolin techniques. The Shaolin Temples provided the necessary secrecy for the development of effective fighting arts, and also the impetus for the spread of such arts throughout China. Shaolin affected the lives of the people it touched, and, in turn, was affected by whoever came to practice it. Physiological and psychological differences among Chinese peoples such as differences that are the result of the varied environments in which they live formed the basis for technically different kinds of shaolin; no less important in the development of shaolin were the political ambitions of emperors and warlords of the time.

Both Shaolin Temples naturally became the loci for secret societies during the time when the Sung dynasty (960–1279) was invaded by barbarians from the north. Two broad movements established the relationship between the Shaolin Temples and secret societies: the White Lotus Society which had influence in North and West China, and the Hung Society with its sphere of activity in West, Central, and South China. Members of these movements are known to have frequented the Shaolin Temples. Though the Shaolin Temples were once essentially religious centers, with the overthrow of the Ming dynasty (1662) by the Ch'ing these temples became politically oriented. Chih Shan, a teacher, came to the Fukien Shaolin Temple to oversee its operations and to establish systematic training in combative arts. Yin Hung-shen, whom members of the Hung Society consider the founder of their organization, died in 1645 after leading an unsuccessful attempt to bolster the declining Ming. Yin chose to use the name of the first emperor of the Ming, Hung-wu, as the name for his society, and made the battle cry "Overthrow the Ch'ing and Restore the Ming" famous. A decade or so later, Fukien Shaolin Temple monks became conspirators, echoed Yin's battle cry, and plotted a revolt against the Manchu. History is vague about the role that the Shaolin Temple monks played in this and other uprisings, but it is logical to assume that monks from both Shaolin Temples participated to a considerable degree in combative activity right up through the

Boxer Rebellion at the beginning of the twentieth century.

Today the Shaolin Temples stand as inactive and lonely relics of the past. They are, however, venerated by all exponents of Chinese hand-to-hand arts who acknowledge the importance of these temples. Through the efforts of the early survivors of the Shaolin Temple massacres, shaolin techniques were widely dispersed. This, in turn, created favorable opportunities for the passing down of combative teachings to others who became interested in this art. And because many thousands of Chinese peoples subsequently migrated to lands such as Taiwan, Hong Kong, the Philippines, Thailand, Indonesia, Singapore, and Malaysia, we of the present generation are able to receive these teachings, albeit often changed from what they originally were.

Some Definitions

It is common for non-Chinese peoples to refer to any and all Chinese hand-to-hand arts as Chinese boxing. This convenient but old-fashioned expression appears to have been coined by the British, but it has never been accepted by the Chinese people. To equate Chinese hand-to-hand arts with boxing methods is to leave untold a substantial portion of the intrinsic nature of the arts. It is true that sparring tactics do exist, and make up a considerable portion of many of the Chinese hand-to-hand systems, but if it becomes necessary to refer to such tactics, the terms *chung-kuo ch'uan* (Chinese fist), *ch'uan-fa* (fist method), or *ch'uan-shu* (fist art) should be used. The facts that sparring tactics never exist alone in any Chinese hand-to-hand art but are coupled with those of a grappling nature and that sparring and grappling tactics are always used in conjunction with a wide range of weapons make it necessary to use a more appropriate term when speaking of Chinese hand-to-hand arts.

Wu shu (martial arts) is used by most modern Chinese people to categorize all the arts of a hand-to-hand nature. But it can be properly argued that even this expression is inappropriate when one speaks of the entire spectrum of Chinese hand-to-hand arts, for there is really very little that is truly martial in the majority of the systems in vogue today. Modern hand-to-hand arts are, at best, methods of scuffling developed by civilians such as merchants and shopkeepers; these arts are not the martial methods of professional warriors or fighting men. Most of the modern systems are geared more toward the promotion of public

health, recreation, physical education, and theatrical per-
formances for the entertainment of an audience, rather than
toward combative ends. Thus the problem of finding an
accurate and acceptable definition that includes all forms
of Chinese hand-to-hand arts, whatever their purposes, is
by no means solved. Perhaps the use of the expression *kuo
shu* (national art), which is used by the mainland Chinese,
is one good way to categorize all Chinese hand-to-hand
arts; *wu shu,* under this definition, is but a subdivision of
those arts, and relates to systems that are devoted to combat.

We hear a lot about *kung fu* today. This popular Cantonese
expression has, through common usage, become synony-
mous with a system of hand-to-hand art. Such usage, however, is highly inaccurate. The expression *kung fu* means
only the dedicated effort that one puts into a task or any
kind of physical effort; thus this expression is a generic term
for action or exercise somewhat skillfully performed, nothing more. Of course an exponent of hand-to-hand arts
who trains assiduously demonstrates *kung fu,* but so do the
hardworking housewife who cleans her house and the
person who paints a picture, polishes an automobile, or
rakes a garden. There is nothing inherently combative or
martial in *kung fu.* The correct use of this expression is
limited to descriptions of domestic or utilitarian skills. The
combative profession refrains from using this term in connection with Chinese hand-to-hand arts. If the professional
must use some term to describe the combative action-skill-
training process, he uses the term *wu kung,* which specifically
refers to a combative endeavor.

Even the most inexperienced exponent of Chinese hand-
to-hand arts knows of the *wai chia* and *nei chia,* the external
and internal families or systems. These terms are traditional
ones, but are often grossly misinterpreted, even by exponents
of the Chinese hand-to-hand arts. Those people who mis-
takenly divide Chinese arts into absolute categories and see
the arts as either external or internal systems draw a clear
line between such forms as shaolin, which represents the
former category, and other systems such as *t'ai chi ch'uan,*
pa-kua, and *hsing-i,* which represent the latter category.

When we carefully examine the orthodox definitions of
external and internal systems, however, we must rely on
what is generally credited to the genius of Chang San-feng,
a Taoist monk who resided at Wu-tang Shan during the
Sung dynasty. Chang is traditionally honored as the origi-

nator of the internal system (*nei chia*). The exponents of shaolin in Chang's day may have been used to an extremely hard or vigorous kind of training routine, perhaps one detrimental to their health. Disheartened by what he saw as an offensive quality in shaolin, Chang devised a more pliable and sensible kind of defensive art; this he termed *nei chia*. Chang also defined external and internal systems. From his definitions it is clear that for him both systems were more alike than different; but he named the development of *ch'i kung*, an intrinsic kind of energy, as a salient part of the internal systems, and made no direct reference to it in connection with external systems. To the original definitions of external and internal systems must be added the fact that shaolin has, since its beginning, been regarded by many as an external system simply because of the legend that makes Ta Mo its originator. Ta Mo was an outsider, a person external to the Chinese family of peoples, while internal systems were so named because they were developed by persons of Chinese blood.

Today, few experienced exponents of Chinese hand-to-hand arts subscribe to the idea that external systems are wholly hard or resistive in nature, and internal systems are totally soft or pliable systems. At this point in history, it is evident to those who have studied both the external and internal arts that the differences between the arts are small ones indeed. Numerous examples exist to prove that internal systems contain rigorous hardness, that of a kind unparalleled in any of the so-called hard external systems, and that the reverse is also true. Most of the hand-to-hand arts that are practiced today are mixtures of what perhaps were once arts that were predominantly either hard or soft in nature, but these distinctions have become so blurred that today it is difficult and of dubious value to insist that existing systems are either one or the other. Some of the changes that have come over original hand-to-hand arts represent the effects of honest human error such as was made in interpreting older teachings, or are the result of equally meritorious attempts by some persons to improve older systems. Other changes were made deliberately to avoid conflict with the traditions of older systems. Still other changes were based on the enterprising nature of certain individuals who used their skills for commercial gain and social prestige. In order to ensure the attainment of such personal aims, many exponents found it necessary to remake traditional hand-to-hand arts so that they would appeal to and draw mass numbers of the modern generation to their training halls.

Northern and Southern Shaolin Systems

Pai are special organizations founded by Chinese exponents of hand-to-hand arts for the purpose of providing systematic control of their arts. No accurate census has been taken of the number of pai, but even if such a census were restricted to those pai that sponsor shaolin systems, the number would probably be in the thousands.

According to orthodox beliefs, shaolin pai fall into two major divisions: those that support Northern Shaolin, and those that make Southern Shaolin the center of their activity. Northern Shaolin is believed to have originated at the Honan Shaolin Temple, while Southern Shaolin is believed to have come from the Fukien Shaolin Temple. In their basic technique patterns, both northern and southern brands of shaolin make use of five animal forms: dragon, snake, crane, tiger, and leopard. Northern Shaolin is traditionally subdivided into three main branches: *Hung,* which stresses physical prowess and the use of strength in a hard or resistive manner; *Kung,* in which clever tactics of a soft or pliable nature offset strength; and *Yue,* in which both hard and soft actions combine to produce technique. From the *Yue* branch of Northern Shaolin there developed systems that depend on the actions of other animals, and even on those of human and supernatural beings: the *Ta-sheng Men,* which makes use of the antics of the monkey; the *Lohan,* or Buddha-like-being system; the *Erh-lang Men,* which is based on the actions of a legendary hero; and the *Wei-t'o Men,* a deity system. Southern Shaolin consists of five main branches: *Ta-hung Men, Liu-chia Ch'uan, Ts'ai-chia Ch'uan, Li-chia Ch'uan,* and *Mo-chia Ch'uan.*

On the basis of the traditional beliefs just summarized, some exponents of shaolin say that there are vast differences between Northern and Southern Shaolin. Exponents of the former type are said to make more use of long-punching actions and to exhibit a higher order of agility, mobility, suppleness, and fluidity of action in the performance of technique than do the exponents of Southern Shaolin. An old adage also states that "Northern Shaolin is 70 percent use of the legs, and 30 percent use of the hands," and posits that the reverse ratio is true for southern types of shaolin.

Here again, as in the case of defining external and internal systems, modern exponents of hand-to-hand arts find it difficult to support such traditional beliefs. It is, of course, possible that the stated differences did once exist between the original forms of shaolin, but such differences have been erased by the effects of time.

If such statements about the ratio of leg usage to hand usage ever were true, they might have reflected primary differences between Chinese peoples living north of the Yangtze and those living to the south of that great river. People in North China are exposed to a harsh environment with the bleak conditions that surround man whenever he chooses to live in a cold climate. Many Chinese in the north live in mountainous regions, and the conduct of their daily lives promotes the development of strong bodies with especially strong legs. Thus, shaolin techniques from North China consist of kicking tactics made with feet protected by footwear; exponents of the northern styles of shaolin are highly motivated to exercise vigorously and thus keep warm. Exponents of Southern Shaolin, however, live in a humid, hot climate where energetic action begets little more than fatigue, and possibly sickness. Nevertheless, peoples of South China are hardworking and make considerable use of their hands and arms, but often go barefoot as they work in rice fields or make their living in other ways in the riverland delta areas of the south. As a result of their tropical environment, the exponents of Southern Shaolin have developed certain physiological and psychological qualities not seen in the Chinese of the north, and these may affect their shaolin techniques. Exponents of Southern Shaolin are conservative in their use of kicking tactics, but it is inaccurate to say that Northern Shaolin is characterized mainly by the use of the legs and that Southern Shaolin depends largely on the use of the hands. This point will become clearer to the trainee when he attempts to practice the fundamental exercises in connection with the stances and postures described in the following chapter.

Fundamentals of Shaolin

—HANDSIGN AND SALUTATION—

Origin and History

Each shaolin pai can be identified by the particular gesture that its exponents make with their hands. There are, therefore, thousands of different kinds of these handsigns in use. In Mandarin the shaolin handsign is called *her chang;* among the Hokkien people, however, the expression *hap chiong* is used.

Both the Mandarin and the Hokkien expressions for the shaolin handsign connote close hands, that is, hands that are held in position together. The handsign that is used in this book applies specifically to the southern kind of shaolin of the Hood Khar pai. It is believed that this handsign is derived from an ancient Chinese Buddhist manner of salutation, and it appears that this handsign was handed down by monk exponents of shaolin to modern practitioners.

Making the Handsign

The shaolin handsign as a gesture is simple enough in its mechanics. To make it, do the following:

1. Stand erect, heels together, toes pointing outward in a natural manner (Fig. 1).

2. Bring both hands together, touching the palms together without undue pressure. Extend each hand's fingers without stiffness and touch the fingers of the other hand. Your hands are now in the close position (Fig. 2).

The shaolin handsign.

3. Keep your shoulders down and relax them as you position both your hands in front of your body at chest level, fingers pointing upward and the fingertips at the level of your throat. Keep your hands about an inch from your body. Keep your elbows in, close to your body, but hold them without stiffness. Look directly to your front (Figs. 3, 4).

Things to avoid.

Inasmuch as it is the goal of a shaolin exponent to be ready at all times to meet any emergency situation that might be thrust upon him by an assailant, it is important for him to avoid practices that would make the shaolin handsign an obstacle to self-defense. You should therefore especially avoid the following:

1. Positioning your close hands in front of your face or at higher levels, such as atop your forehead, since these positions can obscure the movements of your enemy (Figs. 5, 6).

2. Spreading your elbows, thus exposing certain vital parts of your body to a sudden attack (Fig. 7).

24 · SHAOLIN: CHAPTER 2

The handsign and bow.

1

2

FROM ANOTHER ANGLE: Fig. 2

Using the Handsign

The shaolin handsign is commonly used by shaolin exponents in their everyday life, where it serves them as a form of greeting. Execute the handsign as follows:

1. With your hands in the close position in front of your body, bend slowly forward from the waist. Do not bend so low that you cannot see the entire body of a person standing in front of you (Figs. 1, 2). (There are two views of the bowing motion shown in Figure 2. Wherever viewing a motion from another angle will help the trainee get a better idea of correct form, a second view has been provided.)

2. After a brief pause in the low or bowed position, return slowly to an erect posture, keeping your hands in the close position (Fig. 1).

Junior exponents of shaolin often bow to a much lower level than is recommended, especially in deference to a very senior instructor or to an official of their pai, but it is best to follow the instructions detailed here.

The shaolin handsign and bow are used in combination as a formal greeting, a salutation that is an expression of respect to the person or persons the salutation is being rendered to. The handsign is intended to express the wish of the user to avoid conflict. This salutation is always used in shaolin training halls, and all exponents open and close their training exercises with it.

Mental Outlook

The shaolin handsign and the bow are used to provide a moment during which the exponent calms his mind, attains deep breathing, and, in general, reaches a state of overall composure. The fullest benefit from the use of the handsign accrues to the user only when the shoulders are held low, without tension, and the entire body is allowed to hollow naturally at the waist so that the abdominal region protrudes slightly. The chest must not be allowed to rise and fall as if inhaling and exhaling in the manner of chest breathing. Executing the handsign and bow is akin to taking a moment for meditation, during which is engendered an alert and reflective state of mind that prepares one for anything.

—STANCES AND POSTURES—

General

"Stance" refers to the positions of the legs, "posture" to the position of the upper body in relation to stance. In shaolin neither stance nor posture is a static thing, but each is constantly being modified according to the dictates of the situations in which these factors are being used. Stance and posture, especially when used in connection with the displacement of an exponent, are dynamic issues; they are intrinsic elements of shaolin. Each shaolin pai has its own technical requirements for the use of stances and postures in training or combat, and thus the differences are many and very difficult to explain in a description as brief as this. In general, however, the exponents of northern types of shaolin pai prefer stances that depend on a straightened or

locked-out supporting rear leg. Their counterparts, exponents of southern types of shaolin systems, prefer stances in which the rear or supporting leg is curved or locked in a bent position.

An important characteristic of all shaolin systems, northern or southern, is that exponents step to the ground with the heel first on forward displacements; the opposite holds true for a foot used in retreat.

Level-Horse Stance

The most fundamental stance and posture of Hood Khar shaolin is called *ping ma* (Mandarin) or *peh-beh* (Hokkien dialect). The *ping ma* is a level-horse kind of stance. Assume this stance as follows:

1. Execute the shaolin salutation (Figs. 1–3).

2. Shift your weight onto your right leg. At the same time separate your hands but keep them at chest level. Clench both fists (Fig. 4).

3. Step wide *directly* to your left side with your left leg (a distance the equivalent of two and one-half to three times the width of your shoulders). Lower both fists, thumb side up (i.e., knuckles at the bases of the fingers down), to your hips (Figs. 5, 6).

4. As your left foot comes onto the ground, sink down by bending both knees (Fig. 7).

5. Position yourself in a low squatting posture; hold your upper body erect and face directly to the front. Keep your buttocks well under your upper body. Bring both fists to their respective hips in a knuckles-down position (Fig. 8).

Never ignore these keypoints:

1. Step to the final position of your left foot without sliding that foot or adjusting your right platform foot.

2. Position your feet on the same line with your center of gravity, flat on the ground, toes pointing naturally outward.

3. Sink down enough to make your thighs parallel to the ground. This characteristic is called *kuah*.

4. Keep your shoulders down, but relax them.

5. Fill your stomach with strength as you expand it.

6. Sink your weight down evenly (fifty-fifty) between your feet, but do not simply stand on the ground; hold strength downward as if to root yourself to the ground.

The uses of this stance and its corresponding postures in right and left derivatives are detailed on pages 44–46 in connection with basic punching exercises made from this stance. Additional details concerning the use of this stance and its postures in training will be found in Chapter 5.

Assuming the level-horse stance.

5

6

7

8

FROM ANOTHER ANGLE: Fig. 8

1

2

3

Right

Left

Assuming the triangle-horse stance.

7

Triangle-Horse Stance

Another very important basic stance used in the execution of Hood Khar shaolin technique is called *san chiao ma* (Mandarin); Hokkien exponents refer to it as *sakah-beh*. Assume this stance as follows:

1. Complete the shaolin salutation (Fig. 1).
2. Separate your hands and clench your fists, knuckles down, at chest level (Fig. 2).
3. To assume this stance on the right side, shift your weight onto your left leg and slightly bend that knee. Lower your fists, knuckles down, to your hips (Fig. 3).
4. Raise your right leg, bending it at the knee, so that the

thigh is parallel to the ground, or raised at an even steeper angle (Fig. 4).

5. Take a long step forward to your right front corner with your right leg (Fig. 5).

6. As your right foot comes onto the ground, keep your upper body erect, but sink your weight well down so that your right thigh is parallel to the ground (*kuah*). Hold your rear supporting left leg in a locked position, bent at the knee. Maintain your fists in a knuckles-down position at your hips (Fig. 6).

7. To assume a left triangle-horse stance, return to the erect posture shown in Figure 2 and apply the instructions above to your left side (Figs. 7–10).

These keypoints pertain to the triangle-horse stance:

1. Step to the final position of your advanced foot without sliding that foot or adjusting your platform foot.

2. The name of this stance cues the fact that you have advanced one foot *diagonally* forward so that an imaginary triangle is formed. The line between the toes of your advanced foot and the heel of your rear foot is the hypotenuse. The length of your rear foot is one leg of the triangle, and a line connecting the toes of your rear foot with the toes of your advanced foot is the other leg of the triangle. Both feet are flat on the ground; your rear foot is positioned at less than a right angle with your lead foot.

3. Keep the thigh of your advanced leg parallel to the ground (*kuah*) and lock your rear leg in a slightly bent position.

4. Keep your shoulders down, but relax them.

5. Fill your stomach with strength as you expand it.

6. Sink your weight down so that 70 percent is over your advanced leg. Hold the remaining 30 percent over your support leg. Root yourself to the ground by holding strength downward.

7. Look straight ahead, but twist your upper body into a half front-facing posture in the direction of your rear support leg.

The uses of this stance and its corresponding postures in right and left derivatives are detailed on pages 46–53 in connection with basic punching exercises made from this stance. Other information about this stance and its postures is also found in Chapter 5.

Independent-Leg Stance

In Mandarin Chinese this much-used stance is called *han chi su* or *ting su;* Hokkien shaolin exponents refer to it as *ting sik*. All of these expressions connote the idea of a cold chicken since the exponent who assumes this stance stands like a chicken that has positioned itself on one leg and is shivering from the cold. However, throughout the remainder of this book this stance will be referred to as the independent-leg stance. Assume this stance as follows:

1. Execute the shaolin salutation (Figs. 1, 2).

Assuming the independent-leg stance.

2. To assume this stance on the right side, separate your hands, bringing your right hand, palm open and facing down, forward at throat level. Bring your left hand, palm open and facing frontally downward, forward and down to solar-plexus level in front of you. Shift your weight onto your left leg, bending that knee slightly, and sink your weight well down. Keep your upper body erect (Figs. 3,4).

3. Keep your arms and hands in the same relative positions as you raise your right leg, bending it at the knee until that thigh is parallel to the ground (Fig. 5).

4. Lower your raised right leg a bit until the toes of that foot just lightly touch the ground; keep your heel raised off the ground (Fig. 6). This procedure is referred to on the following pages as "floating the leg."

5. Assume the posture shown in Figure 2 and apply the instructions above to your left side.

The following keypoints should be observed in the practice of this stance:

1. Rest 100 percent of your weight on your platform foot. Keep your upper body erect, buttocks held well in as your body sinks straight down over your bent platform leg. Keep your platform foot flat on the ground, toes pointing outward.

2. Keep your shoulders down, but relax them.

3. Fill your stomach with strength as you expand it.

4. Look straight ahead and maintain your upper body in a full front-facing posture in the direction of your floating advanced leg.

5. Keep both arms curved. Hold them with strength, but without stiffness. Concentrate your power in the knife-edge of your leading hand, and in the palm-heel of your nearer hand.

The uses of this stance and its corresponding postures in right and left derivatives are detailed on pages 56–63 in connection with basic kicking exercises made from this stance; its use in training is explained in Chapter 5.

Independent-leg stance on the right.

5   6

FROM ANOTHER ANGLE: Fig. 6

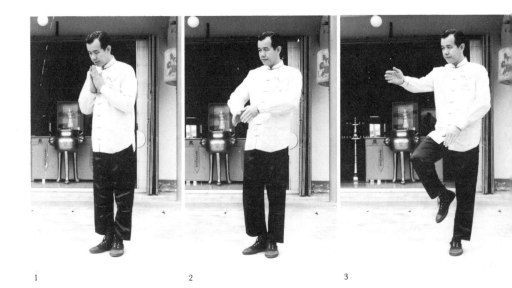

1   2   3

Assuming the high independent-leg stance.

High Independent-Leg Stance

The high independent-leg stance is quite different from the ordinary independent-leg stance as is indicated by its Mandarin name *tu lie chiao* (*tok lip kah* in Hokkien); therefore, it must be studied separately. Assume this stance as follows:

1. Complete the shaolin salutation (Fig. 1).

2. To assume the stance on the right side, shift your weight onto your left leg without bending the knee of that platform leg. Separate and lower both hands to midsection level in front of your body (Fig. 2).

3. Raise your right leg by bending that knee and move your right arm upward, extending it, palm inward (thumb up), in front of your body at chest level. With your left palm cover your midsection in front of your body (Fig. 3).

4. Stand fully erect on your left platform leg as you position your right thigh parallel to the ground, your right foot under your groin, and point the toes of your raised right leg downward. Bend your right elbow enough to position your right hand directly over that elbow, palm inward, at face level in front of you. With your left hand, palm open

4

FROM ANOTHER ANGLE: Fig. 4

and facing forward and down, cover your midsection, close to your body (Fig. 4).

5. To assume a left stance, apply the directions above to your left side.

Study carefully the following keypoints of the high independent-leg stance:

1. Stand with 100 percent of your weight over your platform foot. Do not sink down over that leg. Keep your upper body erect, buttocks directly over the platform foot.

2. Keep your shoulders down, but relax them.

3. Fill your stomach with strength as you expand it.

4. Look straight ahead as you maintain a full front-facing posture in the direction of your raised leg.

5. Hold both arms with strength, but without stiffness. Concentrate your power in the knife-edge of your lead hand and in the palm-heel of your nearer hand.

The uses of this stance and its corresponding postures in right and left derivatives are detailed in connection with the execution of the techniques in Chapters 3 and 4; in Chapter 5 mention is made of its use in connection with training.

1   2   3

Assuming the cat stance.

Cat Stance

The shaolin cat stance is called *mao pu* in Mandarin and *neow poh* in Hokkien. Assume this stance as follows:

1. Complete the shaolin salutation (Fig. 1).

2. To execute this stance on the right side, shift your weight onto your left leg, bending that knee. Raise your right leg, bending that knee until the thigh is parallel to the ground. Move both hands to your left side at chest level (Fig. 2).

3. Take a long step forward with your right leg; separate your hands (Fig. 3).

4. As your right foot comes onto the ground, shift your weight onto that leg and bend that knee (Fig. 4).

5. Slide your trailing left leg forward to bring your left foot, toes pointing outward, directly behind your right heel. At the same time, bring both arms forward, hands open and palms down. Extend your right arm at shoulder level in front of you, palm facing forward and down. Bend your left arm at the elbow to position that palm at solar plexus level, facing forward and down, in front of your body. Sink down over both legs, upper body erect, buttocks well under your upper body (Fig. 5).

6. To assume a left stance, apply the instructions above to your left side.

4

5

FROM ANOTHER
ANGLE: Fig. 5

Familiarize yourself with the following keypoints of this stance:

1. Form a rough outline of the letter **L** with your feet (Fig. 5).

2. Support 90 percent of your weight on your advanced leg. Support the rest of your weight on your trailing leg, with that foot flat on the ground.

3. Keep your shoulders down, but relax them.

4. Fill your stomach with strength as you expand it.

5. Look straight ahead as you twist your upper body into a half front-facing posture in the direction of your rear leg.

6. Hold both arms with strength, but without stiffness. Concentrate your power in the palms of both hands.

The uses of this stance and its corresponding postures in right and left derivatives are detailed in connection with a rapid forward and backward displacement training exercise described on pages 76–80. Additional information about the use of this stance and its postures is found in Chapter 5.

—THE SHAOLIN FIST—

Forming the Fist

Hood Khar pai shaolin trainees are taught to form the fist (*ch'uan* in Mandarin Chinese, *kun* in the Hokkien dialect) in the following manner:

1. Hold your open hand flat, palm up, fingers extended and joined, thumb in contact with the lateral surface of your forefinger (Fig. 1).
2. Bend and roll your fingers into the palm of your hand, curling the palm tightly until no further movement is possible (Fig. 2).
3. Bend and bring your thumb tightly against the outer surfaces of your top two fingers (Fig. 3).

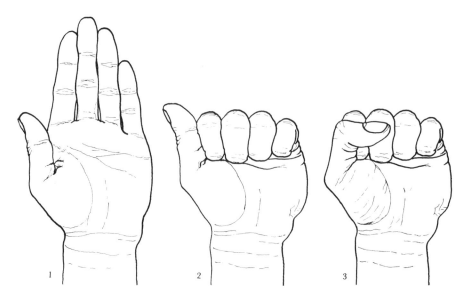

Forming the shaolin fist.

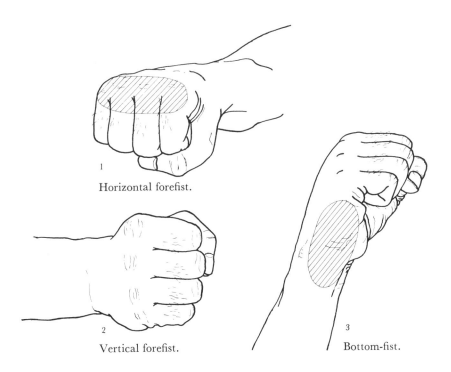

1

Horizontal forefist.

2

Vertical forefist.

3

Bottom-fist.

The Fist as a Striking Surface

The shaolin fist, formed in the manner just described, is used in a variety of ways to deliver the concentrated force of the user's body into a blow that is directed against vital points on an assailant's anatomy. The most commonly used types of fist formations are the forefist (*ch'uan*), the bottom-fist (*siah mien ch'uan*), the back-fist (*ch'uan pay*), and the top-fist (*hu kau ch'uan*).

The forefist may be delivered in either a horizontal or a vertical position (Figs. 1, 2). In either case the exponent makes the entire knuckle area of his fist (shaded area) the striking surface that is to be impacted against a selected target. The horizontally held forefist is best used to strike against hard areas like the ribs, chin, or sternum; the vertically held forefist is best used to strike against fleshy or hollow areas such as the solar plexus, groin, nose, or eyes.

Figure 3 shows the formed bottom-fist with the shaded area representing the area recommended as a striking surface. This kind of fist is best used in hammer-like blows delivered to vital points on the assailant's arms and legs; as such the bottom-fist is a valuable blocking weapon.

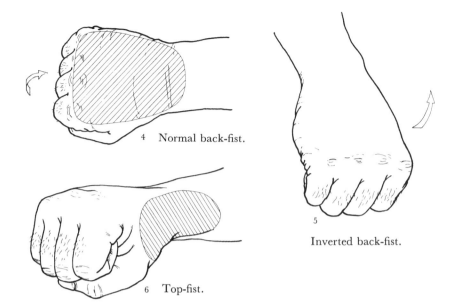

4　Normal back-fist.

Inverted back-fist.

5

6　Top-fist.

Uses for the back-fist are many. It is particularly effective as a blocking weapon when it is used to strike against vital points on an assailant's arms and legs, but it is also useful to deliver direct blows to other body target areas. The back-fist may be used in either normal or inverted-fist fashion (Figs. 4, 5—shaded area indicates the recommended striking surface).

The top-fist is useful in connection with the delivery of roundhouse or hook-punching actions; it also finds limited use as a blocking weapon. Figure 6 shows the formation of the top-fist, and the shaded area is the recommended striking surface.

Delivery of the Shaolin Fist

Two special physical characteristics of the use of the fist identify the true exponent of Hood Khar shaolin. The first of these characteristics concerns the preparatory position of the fist that must precede delivery of long-punching actions. An exponent always brings his fist, knuckles at the bases of the fingers down, to its corresponding hip (Fig. 1). Secondly, from that position at the hip, the exponent always first turns his fist to a knuckles-up or -out position at his hip *before* commencing the delivery of his punch (Fig. 2). No use is ever made of the screwing action of the fist as it moves toward its intended target (Fig. 3).

Delivery of the shaolin fist.

Delivery of the fist in a punching manner is termed *ching*. Two kinds of delivery characterize the Hood Khar use of the fist: *tung keng,* or long-punching actions, and *teh keng,* or short-punching actions. The long punch is best in encounters where the opponent (either a partner in sparring exercises or an opponent in an actual fight) is fairly far from the exponent. The short punch finds great favor among exponents for use in the rapid flurry of punches that can and must be made at very close range with a trainee or an assailant. Long- and short-punching actions are practiced in the form of specific training exercises that follow in this chapter. But not until the fists are specially conditioned are they said to be fully useful as effective weapons of the shaolin-trained exponent; these toughening methods will be described in Chapter 5.

Right punch.   ¹   ²   ³

—BASIC PUNCHING EXERCISES—

Long-Punching Method 1

This exercise combines the coordinated use of stance, posture, and long-punching actions (*tung keng*) made in a forward direction. It is a training method that particularly aids the development of speedy and powerful thrust-punches called *chu ching*, here delivered from a strong and stable level-horse stance (*ping ma*).

Train to deliver this thrust-punch as follows:

1. After completing the shaolin salutation, assume a level-horse stance (Fig. 1).

2. Keep your feet in place, but allow them to pivot as you twist to your left, straightening your right leg somewhat as you push that knee forward and down, while at the same time bending your left knee more. Simultaneously thrust your right fist forward until that arm is fully extended at throat level in front of you. Keep your left fist knuckles down at your hip, but pull that elbow well back as you twist to your left and punch. This is a left level-horse stance (Figs. 2–4).

3. Return to the level-horse stance facing directly forward (Fig. 1). This completes one thrust-punching action.

4. Repeat this thrust-punching action 100 times before returning to the level-horse stance (Fig. 1) to apply the instructions above to making a thrust-punch with your left fist from a right level-horse stance the same number of times (Figs. 5–7).

FROM ANOTHER ANGLE:
Fig. 4

Left punch. (1)

5

6

FROM ANOTHER ANGLE:
Fig. 7

7

Method 2.

The following keypoints of the thrust-punch made from a level-horse stance should be carefully studied:

1. Maintain a deep stance throughout the entire exercise. Keep the thigh of your lead leg (on the opposite side of your punching arm) parallel to the ground (*kuah*). Lock your rear support leg in a bent position, that foot flat on the ground.

2. Keep your feet and your center of gravity on line and your weight evenly distributed between your feet (fifty-fifty).

3. Hold your upper body erect throughout the exercise, twisting it on its vertical axis in a direction that is opposite to the movement of the punching fist. This twist brings your upper body into a half front-facing posture, and drives the shoulder of the punching arm well forward to strengthen the force of that punch.

4. Turn your punching fist to a knuckles-up position at your hip before delivering the punch.

5. Aim your fist inward toward a line parallel to and in front of your body's vertical centerline. At the fullest extension of your punching arm in front of your body your fist should strike an imaginary target on the line.

Long-Punching Method 2

In this training exercise, another method with which to develop a long-punching action, the forward thrust-punch (*chu ching*), is developed in coordination with the lunging action of the triangle-horse stance (*san chiao ma*).

Train to deliver this kind of action as follows:

2   3   4

5   6

1. Complete the shaolin salutation (Fig. 1).

2. Shift your weight fully onto your left leg and raise your right leg by bending that knee, toes pointing downward. Bring that thigh into a position that is parallel to the ground. At the same time, separate your hands, clench them as fists, and position them knuckles down at your hips (Figs. 2, 3).

3. Take a long step forward to your right front corner with your right leg (Figs. 4, 5).

4. As your right foot comes onto the ground, shift your weight well forward over your bent right knee and lunge forward into a right triangle-horse stance (Fig. 6).

Right thrust-punch.

FROM ANOTHER ANGLE:
Figs. 1–8

5. From that stable stance deliver your right fist straight forward at throat level over your lead right leg, your right arm fully extended as your fist strikes an imaginary target in a knuckles-up position. Reinforce that punching action by twisting your upper body to the left and pulling your left elbow well back (Figs. 7, 8).

6. Remain in the right triangle-horse stance, but withdraw your punching right fist in a knuckles-up position to your right hip. Then rotate that fist to a knuckles-down position at that hip. This is one thrust-punching action.

7. Repeat the punching action from the right stance 100 times. Then apply the instructions above to your left side. Execute the thrust-punch from a left triangle-horse stance 100 times.

Keypoints for the thrust-punch made from the triangle-horse stance are as follows:

1. Maintain a parallel-to-ground position with your lead thigh (*kuah*), and maintain the locked-bent rear leg position, that foot held flat on the ground, throughout the exercise.

2. Do not keep your feet and your center of gravity on line. Instead, form the triangle peculiar to this stance (see page 32). Distribute your weight so that 70 percent rests over your lead leg, the remainder over your rear support leg.

3. Hold your upper body erect; you may incline it slightly forward at the time of the contact of the punch with the target. Twist on your vertical axis in a direction opposite to the movement of the fist to attain a half front-facing posture, driving the shoulder of the punching arm well forward and increasing the force of your punch.

4. Turn your punching fist to a knuckles-up position at your hip before delivering the punch.

5. Move your fist directly forward over your lead leg rather than inward toward an extension of your vertical centerline in front of your body at the fullest extension of your punching arm.

1   2

Left uppercut punch.

Short-Punch Training Method

This exercise helps the exponent to develop a powerful and accurate short-punching action (*teh keng*) made in the manner of an uppercut called *chong chui*. Through the use of this exercise the trainee develops a rapid, explosive kind of punching action best delivered from a strong and stable triangle-horse stance (*san chiao ma*) to an opponent at short range.

Train to deliver this short uppercut punch as follows:

1. Complete the shaolin salutation (Fig. 1).
2. Shift your weight onto your left leg, separate your hands, and clench both fists (Fig. 2).
3. Lower both fists, knuckles down, to your hips, and raise your right leg by bending it at the knee until that thigh is parallel to the ground (Figs. 3, 4).
4. Take a long step forward to your right front corner with your right leg (Fig. 5).
5. As your right foot comes onto the ground, assume a right triangle-horse stance. At the same time turn your left fist into a vertical position at your hip (Fig. 6).

3   4   5

6   7   8

6. From a stable stance, and with a sudden burst of speed and power, deliver your left fist, held in a vertical position (back of your hand to your left), in a short uppercut fashion to your front as if striking an imaginary target at solar-plexus level. Do not extend your punching left arm fully. After completing that punch, keep your right fist knuckles down at your right hip (Figs. 7, 8).

7. Remain in a right triangle-horse stance, but withdraw your left fist to your left hip as shown in Figure 6. This completes one punching action.

9   10   11

Right uppercut punch.

8. Repeat this uppercut punching action 100 times. Then apply the instructions above to your other side. Execute the uppercut punch with your right fist from a left triangle-horse stance 100 times (Figs. 9–14).

The keypoints of the short uppercut punch are as follows:
1. Maintain all requirements of a stable triangle-horse stance throughout the exercise, especially the parallel-to-ground position of the lead thigh (*kuah*), and the position of the locked-bent rear support leg.
2. Hold your upper body erect during the entire exercise. Use little of the deliberate twisting of the body on its vertical axis that was called for in the long-punching procedure. Minimizing the twisting action allows for rapid delivery of the short punch.
3. Before delivering the short punch, always turn the punching fist to a vertical position at the hip. The fist should strike the imaginary target in that vertical position. In actual application, however, the fist may also be delivered knuckles up or down.
4. Aim your punching fist directly forward and upward in a short arc from your hip, not inward toward an extension of the vertical centerline in front of your body.

12 13 14

FROM ANOTHER ANGLE:
Fig. 14

—THE SHAOLIN FOOT AND LEG—

Use of the Legs

We saw in Chapter 1 that the old saying "Southern Shaolin is 70 percent use of the arms and hands, and 30 percent use of the legs and feet" can give us a distorted impression as to what shaolin is really all about. To indict southern styles of shaolin as being primarily methods of using hand techniques and northern systems as those that specialize in leg techniques loses validity when shaolin such as that of the Hood Khar pai is analyzed in detail.

Hood Khar shaolin techniques make good use of the legs. Any exponent who trains in the methods of this system quickly comes to realize the importance of the legs in his training. Though the legs are things on which to stand and move during the execution of shaolin techniques, they also have the additional important role of being used as weapons when one deals with an aggressor.

The Foot as a Striking Surface

The foot and leg are used in various combinations to deliver the concentrated force of the user's body into a powerful action made against vital points on an aggressor's body. The most basic uses of the feet include the front thrust-kick, the front snap-kick, and the roundhouse kick.

There are two basic types of front thrust-kicks; both are called *tern chiao* in Mandarin, and *lap kah* in Hokkien. When the shaolin exponent uses the whole flat undersurface of his foot (or shoe), that is, the sole, as a striking surface against a target, the shock generated is not as great as it is when he uses his heel as a striking surface. The former kind of thrust-kick is intended to stun an aggressor or to knock him off-balance rather than to injure him; it is this kind of kick that is usually applied against a training partner. However, when it becomes necessary to injure an assailant, the exponent uses his heel in a thrust-kick fashion; target areas such as the solar plexus, groin, or ribs are commonly impacted in this fashion.

The front snap-kick is also of two types. When the pointed surface of the toes (or shoe) is used as the striking surface, the kick is termed *chuan sing tui;* when the instep is used as a striking surface, the kick is called *liau ing tui.* The former method is best applied against those target areas where it is intended that the shock of the kick penetrate deeply. The most common targets selected to receive this kind of impact are the solar plexus and the heart area. When the instep is used as a striking surface, target areas that are intended to be crushed flat are selected; included here are the groin, or the face or throat of a foe who has been knocked to the ground.

Sau chiao is a name that refers to the roundhouse, or hook, sweep, and sickle kinds of kicks made by the shaolin exponent; either the heel or the instep may be used as a striking surface to both moderately high and low target areas. Only the basic kind of roundhouse kick, one in which the instep is used as a striking surface, is considered in this book.

Delivery of the Foot

Hood Khar kicking techniques are typically southern in nature in that they are more conservative than are most of the kicking tactics used in the northern style of shaolin. This means that the Hood Khar kicking actions are delivered only to moderately high or to low-level target areas. This is done not only to effect a minimum time of delivery for the kick, but also to avoid the great possibility of counterattack that arises when a kicking leg is raised high to reach target areas on the assailant's upper body.

The basic kicking methods that are shown in this book are, therefore, limited to the following target areas:

1. Front thrust-kick: no higher than the opponent's solar plexus
2. Front snap-kick: no higher than the opponent's heart area
3. Roundhouse kick: no higher than the opponent's rib area

Other technical considerations made in connection with kicking actions will be noted in the training exercises that follow where they amplify the performance of those important skills.

1   2   3

Front thrust-kick.

—BASIC KICKING EXERCISES—

Kicking Method 1

This is a drill for learning how to deliver a front thrust-kick (*tern chiao*); it requires no displacement of the body. Aside from learning the actual mechanics of kicking to the front, the exponent also develops the necessary flexibility and strength in his lower back and hips, as well as in the fixation muscles of his platform leg. It is this flexibility and strength that make the use of this kicking action effective.

Perform the front thrust-kick drill as follows:

1. Complete the shaolin salutation (Fig. 1).
2. Assume a left independent-leg stance (*han chi su*), positioning your open hands in front of your body, palms facing down to your front. Extend your left arm, elbow slightly bent, at chest level, and hold your right arm, elbow well bent, close to your body. Cover your solar plexus with your right hand (Figs. 2, 3).

4   5   6

3. Raise your left leg until that thigh is parallel to the ground or at an even steeper angle pointing up (Fig. 4).

4. Maintain an erect posture over your low stance and keep your relative arm and hand positions as you flex your left ankle to make that heel jut downward. Deliver a front thrust-kick with your left leg, that foot contacting an imaginary target at groin level in front of you. Extend that leg to its fullest and use the sole or heel of the left foot as a striking surface (Figs. 5, 6).

5. Retract your kicking left leg to the position shown in Figure 4. This is one kicking action.

6. Repeat the same kick at least fifty times, trying not to touch your left foot to the ground. Then assume a right independent-leg stance and kick in a similar fashion with your right leg fifty times.

FROM ANOTHER ANGLE: Figs. 1–6

Keypoints in the execution of the front thrust-kick follow:

1. Maintain a low stance over a well-bent platform leg throughout this exercise. Lock the ankle of your platform leg to achieve sufficient stability.

2. Keep your posture erect during the kick. However, you may round your back somewhat.

3. Do not push your hips forward at the fullest extension of your kicking leg.

Kicking Method 2

This drill is executed in the manner of the previous kicking exercise, except that here the instep is used as a striking surface. Depending on whether it is made with the point of the toes or with the instep as a striking surface, this kick is called the *chuan sing tui* or the *liau ing tui,* and becomes a front snap-kick. Because of its great similarity to the method just described, it is not illustrated here. One key difference, however, between the front thrust-kick and the front snap-kick is that in the latter type of kick the kicking leg is speedily withdrawn, foot under the body, or the exponent steps to the ground with it immediately after the leg has made contact with its intended target.

Kicking Method 3

This is one of the most fundamental drills in Hood Khar shaolin training methods. It is referred to in Mandarin Chinese as *pai pu kung* (100-steps exercise) and in Hokkien as *pah poh kang*. Through the coordinated action of body displacement and the use of the front snap-kick action (*chuan sing tui*), the trainee using this drill builds strength in his legs, improves his balance and stability in static and moving positions, and gains a powerfully accurate kicking action during his forward movement.

Perform the front snap-kick drill on the move as follows:

1. Complete the shaolin salutation (Fig. 1).
2. Assume a left independent-leg stance (*han chi su*), positioning your arms in front of your body. Extend your left arm, slightly bent at the elbow, hand open, and palm facing down to your front at chest level. Hold your right arm, elbow well bent, nearer your body, palm open and facing down to your front to cover your solar plexus (Figs. 2, 3).
3. Maintain your low stance as well as your arm and hand positions as you slowly raise your left leg until that thigh is at least parallel to the ground. Extend your left ankle and point the toes downward (Fig. 4).
4. Deliver a forward snap-kick with your left leg, using the point of the toes as a striking surface (*chuan sing tui*). Fully extend that kicking leg and kick as if to break through a foe's flesh to penetrate his heart (Fig. 5).
5. Step quickly to the ground with your kicking left leg without retracting that leg. Keep your toes pointing out. Assume a left independent-leg stance (*han chi su*) (Fig. 6). This is one step-and-kick action.
6. Continue by delivering a kick made in similar fashion with your right leg as shown in Figures 7 and 8, after which, when you step with that kicking right leg to the ground and assume a right independent-leg stance, you will have completed two step-and-kick actions. Repeat this drill by alternately kicking with the left and right legs until you have taken the required total of 100 steps.

The 100-steps exercise: front snap-kick.

7, 8

FROM ANOTHER ANGLE: 100-steps exercise

These keypoints of the kick-and-displace drill should be borne in mind:

1. Prepare for the kick slowly from a deep stance, but deliver the kick quickly, and then step down with that leg and once again move slowly in preparation for the next kick. Do not bob up and down as you move forward.

2. Use your hands in a soft fashion, without stiffness, as though you were feeling your way or looking for a target in the dark; keep your fingers extended and joined.

Leg-Strengthening Exercise

In the development of a shaolin exponent there can be no compromise made with the necessity to develop and maintain leg flexibility and strength. The training regimen of the Hood Khar pai contains a special drill that clearly supports the emphasis that is placed by exponents of this southern style of shaolin on the use of the legs. In Mandarin Chinese the exercise is called *fu tui* (to squat low); in Hokkien it is known as *pok tui*. Though this drill is not a kicking exercise, it is always performed in conjunction with training the legs for kicking. It is specifically used to stretch and make flexible the legs and the waist regions. Through a coordinated effort of stepping while stooping low, pivoting and turning, and repetitive displacement of the body, the exponent using this drill develops tremendous strength in his lower body. An additional benefit derived from this drill is that it prepares the trainee's leg and waist muscles to support fast and powerful kicking actions of an advanced nature.

There are two ways in which this drill can be performed. One method is designed for the novice trainee, the other for more advanced trainees.

If you are a novice trainee begin this drill by attempting to make fifty step-and-turn actions in the following manner:

1. Complete the shaolin salutation (Fig. 1).

2. Take a wide step directly to your left with your left leg, and assume a left level-horse stance (*ping ma*). Bring both fists to your hips in a knuckles-down position (Figs. 2–4).

3. Allow your right leg to straighten and the heel of that foot to rise as you shift your weight fully onto your bent left leg (Fig. 5).

4. With your right leg step closely behind your platform left leg. Maintain an erect posture and keep your fists at hip level, but touch your stepping right foot, toes to the ground, behind your left foot to assist you in keeping your balance (Fig. 6).

5. Restep with your right foot more deeply around behind you to your left. Keep your platform left leg in place, but turn your body to the right as you step (Figs. 7, 8).

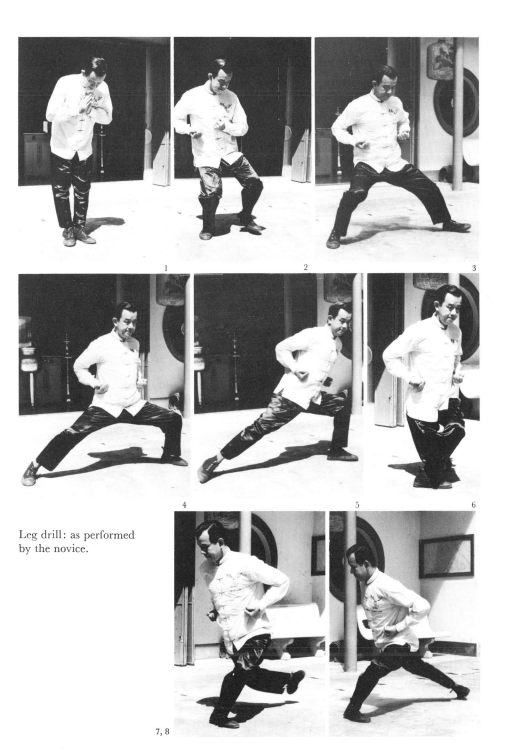

1   2   3

4   5   6

Leg drill: as performed
by the novice.

7, 8

9   10

6. When your right foot comes onto the ground, continue turning your body to the right and come around 180° from your original starting position. Pivot your left foot to accommodate this turn, and lunge well over your right leg to assume a right level-horse stance (Figs. 9, 10). This is one step-and-turn action.

7. Repeat by stepping with your left leg around behind yourself, turning, and assuming the left level-horse stance once again, and so on for a total of fifty movements.

8. Figures 11 to 17 show the continuation of this drill (from the position shown in Figure 10) performed as it would be by an advanced exponent of shaolin. Notice in Figures 12 and 13 that the stepping left foot does *not* touch down to aid balance; rather, it is taken wide around, directly to its final position behind the trainee. Repeat this step-and-turn movement, without the foot-aid to balance, 100 times.

Keypoints in the execution of the leg-strengthening exercise are as follows:

1. This exercise must be done slowly. As its name implies, the *fu tui* places emphasis on obtaining and maintaining a low stance that is characterized by the positioning of the thigh of the lead leg parallel to the ground (*kuah*).

2. In its most advanced form, the *fu tui* provides the exponent with the development of balance and displacement mechanics involving the use of leg actions that are useful in the execution of advanced leg tactics such as the hook and sickle kicks to both low and moderately high target areas.

11

12

13

14

15

Leg drill: as performed
by the advanced.

16, 17

—THE SHAOLIN OPEN HAND AND ARM—

Use of the Hands and Arms

In addition to the fist, which is a very valuable natural weapon for the exponent of shaolin, certain other hand formations and other parts of the arms may also be used as weapons. Like the fists, all of these other anatomical weapons must be specially trained by toughening exercises to endure the forces that are generally present when these weapons make impact with a target (see Chapter 5).

Basic open-hand formations used in this book include use of the palm, the back of the hand, and the knife-edge of the hand; parts of the arm used are the flexed top portion of the wrist, the outer, inner, and top portions of the forearm, and the elbow.

Delivery of the Open Hand

The iron palm is traditionally reported to be the favorite weapon of a shaolin exponent. Special training methods, such as those shown in Chapter 5, make the open hand tough and durable. In this book, however, we are concerned with basic uses of the open palm, and, as such, all descriptions herein are limited to uses of the palm as a cover or protective shield for the vital parts of the user's anatomy, and to explanations of the role of the open palm in covering and controlling the assailant's arm and hand actions (*tah*) (Figs. 1, 2).

When the knife-edge of the hand (*che*) is used as a striking surface it can be delivered in a backhand or normal trajectory to the target (Figs. 3, 4). It may also be used in slicing-block fashion to break contact with an assailant (Fig. 5).

The hard top portion of a flexed wrist is best used in split-block (*tiau*) fashion to deflect an aggressor's punching arm upward or outward, away from its intended target (Fig. 6).

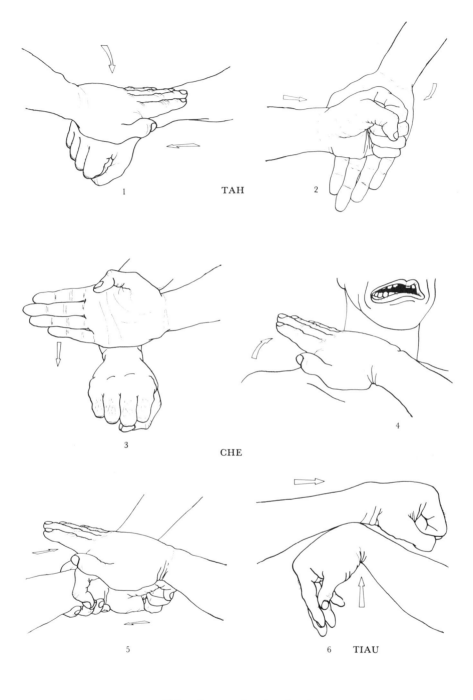

1   TAH   2

3   CHE   4

5   6 TIAU

Using the open hand and wrist.

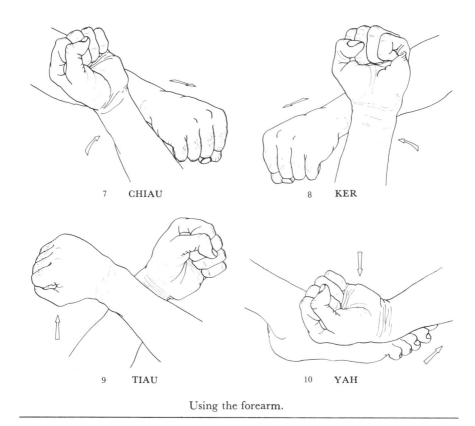

| 7 | CHIAU | 8 | KER |
| 9 | TIAU | 10 | YAH |

Using the forearm.

A foe's attacking arm or leg can readily be blocked by use of the forearm. Direct use of the outside block (*chiau*) makes the outer edge of the forearm the striking surface; this block is applied by moving the arm in ordinary trajectory across the body from the outside. The inside block (*ker*) applies the inner edge of the forearm as a striking surface in a backhand kind of trajectory across the body to the outside. The rising block (*tiau*), in which the outer edge of the forearm becomes the striking surface, rises vertically in front of the body with the blocking arm assuming an acute angle with the vertical. When the top portion of the forearm is used as a striking surface to block a foe's attacking member down, this block is termed *yah* (Figs. 7–10).

Specific uses of the open hand and arm will be described in connection with the techniques in Chapters 3 and 4. The following training exercises complement the execution of those actions in the techniques.

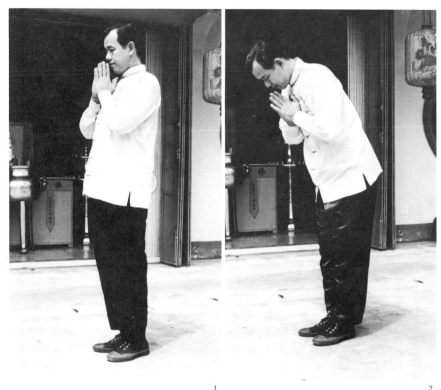

The shaolin salutation.

1   2

White Crane Exercise

This exercise gives the trainee the means by which to strengthen and make stable his entire body in connection with the application of an explosive, oscillatory, or vibrating kind of energy release such as is used to shake off an enemy's grip, or to shove or bump him off-balance. This exercise also coordinates arm, hand, and body actions toward such ends. Mandarin Chinese call this exercise *pai her liang tsu;* Hokkien exponents call it *pei hok kwi sit.* Both expressions suggest a white crane spreading its wings.

Perform the crane exercise as follows:

1. Complete the shaolin salutation (Figs. 1, 2).

3   4

Performing the white crane exercise.

2. Assume a right independent-leg stance (*han chi su*). Extend both arms forward and down to waist level, separating your hands and turning the palms upward as you come into that stance (Figs. 3, 4).

3. Without a pause, slowly raise both arms sidewards and upwards, flexing your wrists and allowing the palms to turn down. As your arms come to a position above shoulder level, step forward to your right front corner with your right leg, and, with a sudden burst of speed and power, shift your weight onto your right leg, lunging well forward into a right triangle-horse stance (*san chiao ma*). At the same time, fling both arms circularly over and forward with a snap (like the arm action in the butterfly breaststroke) to your front, turning your palms outward as your hands arrive a shoulder width apart, arms fully extended, high above your head to your front (Figs. 5–7).

4. Continue by relaxing your body and slowly shifting your weight back onto your left foot. Bring your advanced right foot back on line with your platform left foot, and, at the same time, withdraw your arms and bring both hands together at chest level in front of you (Fig. 8). This is one wing-spreading movement.

5. Repeat this movement fifty times. Figures 9 to 13 show the second movement, after which you must return to the position shown in Figure 8. Then perform a similar series of actions from a left independent-leg stance, using your right leg as a platform leg.

Observe the following keypoint when performing the crane exercise:

Develop a snap action in the forward portion of this exercise. You must produce a distinct sound at this point, that sound coming from your body, not from your garment. If you fail to make this sound, practice more.

9 10 11

12 13

White crane exercise: second movement.

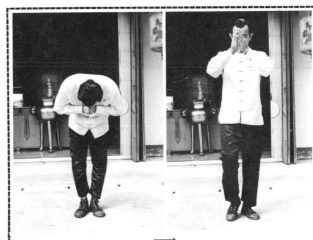

FROM ANOTHER ANGLE:
Figs. 2–7

Performing the fast-hands exercise.

1   2

Hand-and-Arm Coordination Exercise

Mandarin Chinese exponents of shaolin call this exercise *kwai shou,* while Hokkien adepts call it *kuai chiu;* both expressions imply fast hands. The fast-hands exercise is invaluable in teaching the exponent how to coordinate rapid actions of his hands and arms with powerful forward displacements such as are useful in carrying the attack to the assailant. Through this exercise the trainee develops the accurate transmission of the power of his body against a foe. There are two ways of performing this exercise. The first involves an oscillatory kind of action and is designed for use by novices; the second, a repetitive forward displacement kind of action, is preferably used by advanced exponents of shaolin.

If you are a novice trainee perform the fast-hands exercise as follows:

1. Complete the shaolin salutation (Fig. 1).
2. With a sudden burst of speed and power, take a very long step forward with your right leg (literally jump forward), and at the same time fling both arms forward and upward, hands open, palms down (Figs. 2, 3).
3. As your right foot comes onto the ground, bring your trailing left leg up behind it and assume a right cat stance (*mao pu*). Extend both arms, elbows slightly bent, in front of your body, your right arm uppermost and at face level and

3   4

5   6

your right hand farthest from your body, your left arm, elbow well bent, held in close to your body, that hand covering your solar plexus (Fig. 4).

4. Retreat by relaxing your whole body and taking a long step backward with your left leg, sliding your advanced right leg up close to the now platform left leg. Bring your hands back, elbows well bent, with your hands once again covering the same relative parts of your body as they did on the forward move. Assume the right cat stance once again (Figs. 5, 6). This is one complete movement.

7

8

Forward displacement
sequence.

9

10

5. Figures 7 to 10 show another forward displacement portion of this exercise, after which you must return to the position in Figure 6 to complete the second movement.

6. Repeat this action, going forward and backward in an oscillatory fashion, but perhaps gaining a bit of ground forward each time you move in that direction. Repeat this 100 times before performing this exercise from a left cat stance the same number of times.

7. If you are an advanced exponent of shaolin, perform this exercise by making five forward displacements and arm-and-hand actions in succession before returning to your original starting position, that accomplished also by withdrawing in five successive retreating movements.

FROM ANOTHER ANGLE: Figs. 1–10 (continued on following page)

The keypoints of the fast-hands exercise follow:

1. To maintain the rhythm of this exercise, make forward movements with a sudden burst of speed and power. These moves are a hard kind of action. However, perform movements of retreat and recovery at a much slower pace and with the body relaxed, for these are soft actions.

2. When performing the novice, or oscillatory, movement, move your body to and fro, as if it were a wave washing up on a beach and then running out at ebb. In the advanced drill, seek to reduce the time lag between individual forward movements.

少林 **3**

The Lohan Pattern

General

One of the bases for both northern and southern styles of shaolin is the spirit and actions that are attributed to the *Lohan*. The Lohan was originally a bandit type of character who roamed freely over the Chinese countryside making his living by device and sheer cunning. Stealing, lying, and cheating, the Lohan included the worst possible traits in his personal character. Foul play was the Lohan's specialty, making him truly a professional thug.

Traditional legends tell how a certain notorious Lohan was befriended by a Chinese Buddhist monk and given food and shelter. Impressed with the hospitality and generosity of the monk, the Lohan determined to mend his bad ways. He undertook a complete personal reform. He studied such academic subjects as religion and philosophy and eventually became an honest and upright citizen. Today, Chinese still revere this Lohan as a man of scholarly and religious attainment and admire his put-down-the-sword-and-turn-to-prayer action. Below is a short summary of the religious significance of the Lohan. This explanation may help the modern shaolin exponent appreciate the importance of the Lohan to shaolin teachings.

Chinese Buddhism recognizes three types of spiritually perfected beings: (1) Buddhas, who perceive the truth for themselves and teach it to others, (2) Pratyeka-Buddhas, or private Buddhas, who perceive truth but keep it to themselves, and (3) Arhats, or Worthies, who learn the truth from others, but realize it only for themselves. In Mandarin Chinese, the Arhat is called Lohan.

The Lohan belongs to the third class of the Buddhist hierarchy. He is a being who, through his earnest belief in the teachings of Buddha and his aspiration to become a Lohan, is a perfected form of being for whom there is no rebirth. He already enjoys Nirvana, but will only enter fully into that blissful state after death, with all vestiges of his personality negated. The road to becoming a Lohan is a hard one. This status can only be attained by he who dedicates his life to the attainment of personal virtue based on self-sacrifice. The Lohan is endowed with certain special qualities, such as the Three Insights:

1. Insight into the mortal conditions of Self and others in previous lives
2. Supernatural Insight into future mortal conditions
3. Nirvana Insight into present mortal sufferings, allowing the Lohan to overcome all passions or temptations

But a Lohan also possesses Six Supernatural Powers:

1. Instantaneous view
2. Ability to hear any sound anywhere
3. Ability to know the thoughts of all minds
4. Knowledge of all former existences of Self and others
5. Power to be anywhere or to do anything at will
6. Supernatural Consciousness of the waning vicious propensities

Original Lohan shaolin technique is believed to have consisted of *Shih-pa Lohan Shou* (Lohan eighteen hands). The number of techniques comes from the number of basic exercises attributed to the genius of Ta Mo. The primary purpose of original Lohan technique was to provide monks with a method of self-practice by which their general health could be improved. Through the use of the Lohan technique, monks sought to strengthen their minds for the difficult task of meeting the rigid discipline that was expected of them. But the Lohan system was not without value as a system of self-defense. In this chapter the Lohan system of the Hood Khar pai is presented as an exercise in aiding the development of a sound mind and a healthy body; in Chapter 4 the self-defense aspects of the Lohan system will be explored.

Ii tao is a Mandarin expression used to connote a prearranged pattern of action that is used by exponents of shaolin to train themselves in a particular way for the purpose of maintaining health, and also as a basis for more advanced applications in self-defense. The pattern method of training (*ii tao*) is used by all shaolin systems. In the Hood Khar pai it consists of two types: (1) solo practice (*Lohan ch'uan*), in which a lone trainee moves in accordance with a prearranged and coordinated sequence of actions, and (2) partner practice (*Lohan tao ch'uan*), in which two training partners engage each other in a prearranged order of action. In this chapter we are concerned only with the former kind of pattern training method.

Follow the instructions given in the text very carefully, beginning slowly enough so that the proper form of each element of the pattern can be learned. As you increase the skill of your execution of the pattern you may increase the speed of your movement until the entire pattern can be performed smoothly, and the recommended power climaxes appear as they are indicated in the text. As soon as possible, perform the solo Lohan pattern in its entirety at each training session. This requires that you memorize the sequence of actions. When the full pattern can be performed as a series of fluent actions, it should be practiced at least four or five times during each training session.

The photographic illustrations make clear the instructions given in the text, but often, due to the great difficulty of obtaining the right photograph at the right instant, there will be some slight differences between the photographs and the text. When you are in doubt as to which of these is correct, follow the text.

1

1   2   3

THE LOHAN PATTERN

OPENING THE PATTERN
Execute the shaolin salutation (*her chang*) (Figs. 1, 2).

1. Lohan Kai Kung (Lohan Drawing a Bow)

Maintain your hands in the position used for the saluta-tion, but shift your weight onto your right leg, bending that knee, and slowly take a wide step directly to your left side with your left leg (Fig. 3). Sink down into a level-horse stance (*ping ma*) and look directly to your front (Fig. 4). Twist your upper body to the left and slowly shift more weight onto your left leg, allowing your right foot to pivot slightly, heel on the ground. Separate your hands as you twist, the left palm facing down, the right palm facing down to your left side. Both hands should cover the midline areas of your mid-front body (Fig. 5). Sink slowly down until your right knee just touches the ground (Fig. 6). Then, with a sudden burst of speed and power, thrust your left arm straight up over your head with the palm of that hand facing upward, fingers to your rear. At the same time,

84 • SHAOLIN: CHAPTER 3

4

5

6

7

forcefully thrust your right arm straight down in front of you so that the palm faces downward, fingers pointing to the left. Your arms form a vertical line that bisects your body in a longitudinal plane (Fig. 7).

8 9

10 11

2. Chin Pu Chong Ch'uan (Step and Punch)

Rise slowly as you clench both fists and move your right hand up the centerline in front of your body and your left hand down the same centerline. Shift your weight onto your left leg, keeping that knee bent, and take a long step forward with your right leg (Figs. 8, 9). As your right foot comes onto the ground, shift your weight well forward onto that leg and assume a right triangle-horse stance (*san chiao ma*). At the same time, position your right arm, bent at the elbow, across the front of your body at waist level and turn that fist knuckles down. Bring your left fist, knuckles down, to your left hip (Fig. 10). With a sudden burst of speed and power, deliver an uppercut punch (*chong chui*) with your right fist, knuckles down, at stomach level to your front (Fig. 11).

3

12

13

14

15

16

3. Sang Pu Swang Chuay (Double Step and Double Punch)

Unclench both fists, but maintain your hands in their relative positions (Fig. 12). Shift your weight onto your advanced right leg and step forward with your left leg. At the same time slowly spread your arms to the sides, palms upward (Fig. 13). Shift your weight onto your advanced left leg, and raise both arms, elbows bent, so that your fists are positioned, knuckles back, at head level on either side of your head (Fig. 14). With a sudden burst of speed and power, step forward with your right leg and bring that foot on line with your left foot. At the same time deliver a double-fist punch (*cha chui*) downward and forward to your front at waist level. Reinforce that punching action by sinking your weight down over slightly bent knees (Figs. 15, 16).

4

17
18

5

19
20
21

4. Te Chiao Hern Tu (Iron Bridge Across a Stream)

Shift your weight over your bent right leg, and turn to your left; unclench your left fist (Fig. 17). With a sudden burst of speed and power, assume a left independent-leg stance (*han chi su*). At the same time snap your left arm, bent at the elbow, up, to deliver a rising split block (*tiau*) with the hard upper portion of your flexed left wrist and outer forearm at head level. Reinforce that blocking action by bringing your right fist, knuckles down, to your right hip (Fig. 18).

5. Hey Hu Chuan Sing (Black Tiger's Paw Strike)

Quickly take a long step forward with your left leg and assume a left triangle-horse stance (*san chiao ma*). Simultaneously, with a sudden burst of speed and power, deliver a forward thrust-punch (*chu ching*) with your right fist, knuckles up, at chest level. Reinforce that blow by twisting your upper body to the left and withdrawing your left arm,

6

22

23

24

25

bent at the elbow, hand held as a fist, knuckles back, to a position that covers your forehead (Figs. 19–21).

6. Lohan Yee Ting (Lohan Moving a Frying Pan)

Begin to turn 180° to your right by shifting your weight onto your left leg and pivoting on both feet. At the same time, unclench both fists. Bring your right arm, bent at the elbow, hand palm down, around across the front of your body at face level as you turn. Simultaneously, lower your left arm, bent at the elbow, palm down (Figs. 22, 23). With a sudden burst of speed and power, complete your turn and assume a right independent-leg stance (*han chi su*). Use the knife-edge of your open right hand in a sweeping-block (*chiau*) fashion to your right, as your left hand, palm down, covers your midsection. Maintain the right independent-leg stance; flex both wrists. Extend your right arm, bent at the elbow at face level. Cover your solar plexus with your left hand close to your body (Figs. 24, 25).

26

27

7. Yu Chuan Sing Tui (Kick To Pierce the Heart)

While standing in the right independent-leg stance raise your right leg, bending it at the knee until that thigh is parallel to the ground, toes pointing downward, and thus assume the high independent-leg stance (*tu lie chiao*). Maintain your relative arm and hand positions (Fig. 26). With a sudden burst of speed and power, deliver a forward snap-kick (*chuan sing tui*) with your right leg, using the toes as a striking surface aimed at heart level (Fig. 27).

8. Tui Pu Chey Chang (Step and Slice)

After delivering the kick, retract that leg quickly and step sideward to your right onto the ground. Maintain your relative arm and hand positions (Fig. 28). As your right foot comes onto the ground, shift your weight onto that leg and turn 90° to your left. Float your advanced left leg. At the same time turn your right hand palm upward and bring that arm, extended but slightly bent, in front of your body at chest level. Clench that fist. Simultaneously position your left hand, palm down, near your right shoulder,

8   28   29

30   31

and on top of your right arm (Figs. 29, 30). With a sudden burst of speed and power, make a cutting motion with the knife-edge of your open left hand. Move the hand forward and down across the undersurface of your right arm to use the knife-edge of that hand in a slicing-block (*che*) action at groin level. Reinforce this blocking action by shifting fully onto your rear right leg to assume a left independent-leg stance (*han chi su*) and, at the same time, forcefully withdraw your right arm to bring that fist, knuckles down, to your right hip (Fig. 31).

32   33   34

9. Ching Kan Toh Yueh (Support the Moon)

Take a long step backward with your advanced left leg. At the same time, keep your right fist at your right hip, but raise your extended left arm, palm down, to shoulder level in front of you (Fig. 32). Shift your weight onto your now retreated left leg and bend that knee while turning to your left. Extend your right arm forward, hand held as a fist, and bring that arm up to head level in front of you as you rotate the fist knuckles up. At the same time, clench your left fist and bring that arm back and down so that you cover your groin with your fist (Fig. 33). Continue without a pause, and, with a sudden burst of speed and power, assume a right high independent-leg stance (*tu lie chiao*). At the same time, cut down and back with your right bottom fist (*siah mien ch'uan*) and outer forearm in a circular arc in scooping-block (*chiau*) fashion in toward your body at stomach level. Reinforce that blocking action by swinging your left arm, hand held as a fist, up overhead (Figs. 34–36).

10. Hern Ch'uan Chuan Sing (Step Forward and Strike)

Take a long step forward onto your right leg, and shift your weight onto that leg to assume a right triangle-horse stance (*san chiao ma*). Simultaneously bend your left arm and lower that fist, rotating it knuckles down, until it is in front of your body at solar plexus level. Bring your right

35

36

10

37

38

39

fist, held in a vertical position, in front of your body to cover your solar plexus (Figs. 37, 38). As you come into the right triangle-horse stance, deliver, with a sudden burst of speed and power, a forward thrust-punch (*chu ching*) to chest level with your right fist held in a vertical position. Reinforce that blow by twisting your hips to the left and withdrawing your left fist to your left hip (Fig. 39).

FROM ANOTHER ANGLE: Figs. 39–45

11

40   41   42

11. Lohan Chi Ku (Lohan Hitting a Drum)

Turn 180° to your left by pivoting on both feet in that direction. Simultaneously hold your left arm, bent at the elbow, fist turned knuckles up, across the front of your body at stomach level, while your right arm, elbow bent, is positioned so that the fist is at your right hip, knuckles down (Figs. 40, 41). With a sudden burst of speed and power, shift your weight well forward and assume a left triangle-horse stance (*san chiao ma*). At the same time, deliver an overhand arc-punch (*yang chiew*) on a diagonal course forward with the back-fist of your left hand at head level in

43　　　　　　　　　　44　　　　　　　　　　45

front of you (Figs. 42, 43). Take a long step forward with your right leg; carry your right arm, hand held as a fist, forward, and fold that arm across your mid-body so that the fist is knuckles out; withdraw your left arm, elbow bent, so that the fist is at your left hip, knuckles down (Fig. 44). As your right foot comes onto the ground, shift your weight well forward with a sudden burst of speed and power and assume a right triangle-horse stance. At the same time, deliver your right bottom-fist in an overhand arc-punch diagonally forward to head level in front of you. Keep your left fist at your left hip (Fig. 45).

12

46 47 48

12. **Ching Kan Fu Hu** (The Emperor Controls the Tiger)

With a sudden burst of speed and power, turn 180° to your left by pivoting on both feet and assume a left independent-leg stance (*han chi su*). As you come into this stance, raise your right arm overhead, hand held as a fist, knuckles back, elbow bent. Simultaneously place your left fist, knuckles down, thumb facing your body, on top of your advanced left thigh (Figs. 46–48).

13. **Lohan Cho Hu** (The Lohan Sits on the Tiger)

Take your left leg back a long step, toes pointing to your left. Simultaneously unclench your left fist, turn the open hand palm down, and use that hand to cover your groin area. At the same time, begin to move your right arm forward, hand held as a fist, knuckles up, extending that arm at head level in front of you (Fig. 49). With a sudden burst of speed and power, shift your weight onto your rear bent left leg and assume a right independent-leg stance (*han chi su*). Simultaneously cut downward with your right arm and back in toward your body to deliver a scooping block (*chiau*) with the outer surface of the forearm and bottom-fist at groin level. Fold that arm, bent at the elbow, across the front of your body at stomach level. Reinforce that blocking action by flinging your left arm, hand held as a fist, knuckles to the rear, up overhead (Fig. 50).

13

49

50

14

51

52

14. Swang Loong Chu Hai (Double Dragon Goes Out to Sea)

Quickly take a long step forward with your right foot, at the same time lowering your left arm, bent at the elbow, hand held as a fist, knuckles up, to chest level. Your right fist and bent arm covers your midsection (Fig. 51). As your right foot comes to the ground, shift your weight onto that leg with a sudden burst of speed and power and assume a right triangle-horse stance (*san chiao ma*). Simultaneously deliver a forward double-punch (*ping chui*). Thrust-punch at chest level with your right fist held in a vertical position, and make an overhead arc-punch, thumb down, with your left fist at head level (Fig. 52).

53 54 55

FROM ANOTHER ANGLE: Figs. 55–58

15. Ting Su Yang Ch'uan (Instant Block and Strike)

Quickly shift your weight back over your bent left leg
and assume a right independent-leg stance (*han chi su*). At
the same time, lower your left arm, hand held as a fist,
knuckles up, bending that arm at the elbow so as to fold
that arm across the front of your body at stomach level
(Figs. 53, 54). Without a pause, with a sudden burst of
speed and power and while maintaining the right independent-leg stance, deliver an overhand arc-punch (*yang
chiew*) with your right back-fist at face level in front of you.
Reinforce that blow by withdrawing your left fist, knuckles
down, to your left hip (Fig. 55).

56   57   58

16. Pai Yuen Ching Tao (White Monkey Plucks Fruit)
Step deeply to your rear with your right foot, turning
your body to the right as you move. While turning, withdraw your right arm across your body at shoulder level,
rotating your right fist knuckles up. At the same time bring
your left arm, hand held as a fist, knuckles up, across the
front of your body at stomach level (Figs. 56, 57). Assume
a right triangle-horse stance (*san chiao ma*) and, with a
sudden burst of speed and power, deliver your right inverted
fist (back of the hand out to your front) in thrust-punch
fashion diagonally downward to your rear at groin level.
Reinforce that blow by flinging your left arm, hand held as
a fist, knuckles back, high overhead to your front. With
this blow, turn your head to the right (Fig. 58).

59   60   61

17. Erh Hu Chu Tung (Hungry Tiger Searching for Food)

Shift your weight onto your bent left leg, but maintain your relative arm and hand positions from the previous technique (Fig. 59). Stand fully on your left leg. Bring your right foot under your body, toes pointing downward, by bending that knee and raising the leg until the thigh is parallel to the ground to assume a right high independent-leg stance (*tu lie chiao*). At the same time, fold your right arm, hand held as a fist, knuckles up, across your body at chest level; unclench your left fist and begin to lower that arm (Fig. 60). Jump in place onto your right leg. As you jump, relax your fists, lower your left arm, hand palm up, to hip level, and extend your right arm, palm down, to face level in front to you. As your right foot comes onto the ground reclench your fists, the right fist, knuckles down, extended in front of you at face level, and the left fist, knuckles up, held farther back and rising to chest level (Figs. 61, 62). With a sudden burst of speed and power, step down with your left foot, float that foot, and assume a left independent-leg stance (*han chi su*). At the same time, deliver a short jab-punch (*twan ch'uan*) with your left fist at face level, knuckles up, but do not fully extend that arm. Reinforce that blow by withdrawing your right fist to your right hip, knuckles down (Fig. 63).

62

63

18 64   65   66

18. Tui Pu Ta Hu (Retreat and Strike the Tiger)

Maintain the relative arm and hand positions of the last technique, keeping strength in your left arm by pressing the arm down. With your left leg step around close behind your platform right leg, and take a deep step to your right rear corner (Fig. 64). Turn 90° to your left and assume a cat stance (*mao pu*). At the same time, raise your right arm, bent at the elbow, hand held as a fist, knuckles back, overhead on your right side. Simultaneously withdraw your left arm across the front of your body, hand held as a fist, knuckles up, at stomach level (Fig. 65). Turn to your left by pivoting on both feet, shift your weight over your bent left leg, and assume a left triangle-horse stance (*san chiao ma*). At the same time, with a sudden burst of speed and power, deliver a downward scooping block (*chiau*) with your right bottom-fist and the outer edge of that forearm at groin level, cutting back and in toward your body with that arm. Fold that arm across your body at stomach level. Reinforce that block by flinging your left arm, hand held as a fist, knuckles back, overhead and back (Fig. 66).

19

67   68

19. **Fan Sao Chi Tui** (Strike Inner Arm)

Withdraw your advanced right leg and float that foot. Assume a right independent-leg stance (*han chi su*). At the same time, lower your left arm, hand held as a fist, knuckles out, and position that arm across your body at stomach level. Simultaneously raise your right arm to chest level, elbow bent and pointing forward, knuckles of that fist turned out (Fig. 67). Maintain your independent-leg stance, but, with a sudden burst of speed and power, deliver an overhand arc-punch (*yang chiew*) with your right back-fist at biceps level to your front; reinforce that blow by withdrawing your left fist, knuckles down, to your left hip (Fig. 68).

20

69

70

21

71

20. Ching Kan Tuan Chiu (Emperor Using Elbow)

Keep your left fist at your hip as you step forward with your right leg in a sudden burst of speed and power to assume a right triangle-horse stance (*san chiao ma*). As you come into this stance, deliver a forward elbow strike at chest level with your right elbow (Figs. 69, 70).

21. Ching Kan Pu Min (Emperor Strikes the Tiger's Face)

Without a pause, deliver an overhand arc-punch (*yang chiew*) at face level to your front with your right back-fist (Fig. 71).

72   73

22. Chuan Sun Chiao Nan (Emperor Strikes the Gate)

Shift your weight onto your bent right leg, step wide to
your left with your left leg, and, with a sudden burst of
speed and power, assume a right level-horse stance (*ping ma*).
As you move deliver an outside block (*chiau*) using the outer
edge of your left forearm at face level in front of you. Rotate
that fist to a knuckles-forward position as you make that
block; reinforce that blocking action by twisting your body
to your right and withdrawing your right arm to bring that
fist, knuckles down, to your right hip (Figs. 72–75).

23. Hey Hu Toh Sing (Black Tiger Steals the Heart)

Keep your feet in place, but pivot on them with a sudden
burst of speed and power to twist your body hard to your
left and assume a left level-horse stance (*ping ma*). At the
same time deliver a right thrust-punch (*chu ching*) at chest
level with that fist; reinforce that blow by withdrawing your
left fist, knuckles down, to your left hip (Figs. 76, 77).

74

75

23

76

77

24

78

79

80

25

83

84

24. **Ching Kan Chong Chui** (The Emperor Wields a Hammer)

Begin to withdraw your right arm, bending that elbow, and rotate that fist knuckles down. Without a pause, shift your weight back over your right leg and assume a right level-horse stance (*ping ma*). Continue to withdraw your right arm, and begin to move your left arm forward, hand held as a fist (Figs. 78, 79). From a right level-horse stance bring both fists to your front at chest level, knuckles up (Fig. 80). With a sudden burst of speed and power, deliver a short jab-punch (*twan ch'uan*) with your left fist, knuckles up, to your front at face level. Do not extend your left arm fully during the punch. Reinforce that blow by twisting hard to your right and withdrawing your right fist, knuckles down, to your right hip (Figs. 81, 82).

81

82

85

86

87

25. **Ching Kan Chiang Moh** (The Emperor Controls an Evil Spirit)

Keep your arms and hands in the relative positions of the last technique as you shift your weight onto your bent left leg (Fig. 83). As your weight comes fully onto your left leg raise your right leg so that that thigh is parallel to the ground and that foot comes under your body. Quickly jump backwards onto your right leg and raise your left leg, bent at the knee, until that thigh is parallel to the ground and that foot is under your body. As your right foot reaches the ground, release a sudden burst of speed and power and, with your left arm, make a cutting motion downward and back in toward your body, using the outer edge of your forearm in a scooping-block (*chiau*) fashion at groin level in front of you. Reinforce that blocking action by flinging your right arm, hand held as a fist, knuckles back, up overhead (Figs. 84–87).

26

88   89

27

90   91

92, 93

26. Mung Hu Ju Tung (A Fierce Tiger Returns to Its Den)

Maintain the relative arm-and-hand positions of the last technique, and take a deep step behind you with your left leg (Fig. 88). As your left foot comes onto the ground, turn to your left with a sudden burst of speed and power by pivoting on both feet and shifting your weight onto your bent left leg. Assume a left triangle-horse stance (*san chiao ma*). With the turn, and as you come into that stance, deliver a downward scooping block (*chiau*) with your right inverted back-fist at groin level, cutting back and in toward your body with that arm. Fold that arm across your body at groin level, hand held as a fist, knuckles up. Reinforce that blocking action by flinging your left arm, hand held as a fist, knuckles back, up and back to an overhead position (Fig. 89).

27. Lohan Sun Tien (Lohan Goes to Heaven)

Maintain the relative arm and hand positions of the last technique, but shift your weight evenly over both your legs and assume a level-horse stance (*ping ma*) (Fig. 90). Then, with a sudden burst of speed and power, shift your weight onto your right leg and assume a right level-horse stance. At the same instant, fling your right arm, hand held as a fist, knuckles up and back, upward and back overhead, and also thrust your left arm downward, hand held as a fist, knuckles to your right, in front of you (Fig. 91).

CLOSING THE PATTERN

Shift your weight onto your extended left leg and come to an erect posture by bringing your right foot on line, heels together, with your platform left foot. Bring both your hands together and execute the shaolin salutation (*her chang*) (Figs. 92, 93).

少
林

Applying the Lohan Pattern

General

Though the trainee may master the mechanics and spirit of the solo Lohan pattern (*Lohan ch'uan*), unless he can apply its actions as techniques in defense of his person, he cannot be said to be a fully trained shaolin exponent.

The Lohan pattern as it is performed with a training partner (*Lohan tao ch'uan*) is designed to provide the trainee with responses to realistic situations such as might be imposed upon him by an assailant. While the entire sequence of the pattern is to be performed as an uninterrupted whole, it is often useful to isolate one or more movements from the pattern and to practice them as separate responses to an attack.

In the performance of the partner-practice method certain technical aspects of shaolin are highlighted and can easily be understood. In particular, when the Lohan partner-practice pattern is properly performed, the essentially dual nature of shaolin is revealed to be a blend of soft and hard actions. True shaolin technique is characterized by the use of a soft or pliable kind of defensive action, followed by a hard or resistive kind of action. That the transition from soft to hard must be instantaneous also becomes apparent. It is not enough to simply block an assailant's attack, or to block it and, in time, to counterattack. What is necessary, and what is further the essence of all true shaolin art, is for the exponent to meld his blocking and counterattack actions so that they operate in a flash, without any noticeable time lag between them. In order to exhibit this important characteristic of shaolin technique, the trainee must avoid a distinct and time-consuming cocking action of either his arm or leg as he prepares to punch, strike, or kick.

A high degree of sensitivity to movement made at close quarters is a key feature of shaolin. This means that the trainee must develop a sense of feeling in his hands, so that through contact with his foe he is able to read the next movement his assailant will make. Knowing his assailant's movement, the shaolin exponent is able to unbalance him by attacking ahead of the very instant at which the assailant's technique is being focused. Thus, rather than opposing the assailant's forces once they have been focused, the exponent of shaolin seeks to disrupt them before they reach that critical focus. Master teachers of shaolin sometimes give the following analogy to explain this important facet of shaolin technique: A revolving bicycle wheel can be stopped with one well-directed thrust of a stick into the moving spokes of that wheel. So it must be with the application of shaolin technique. The hands of an assailant, however fast they may be, must be stopped with one action of the defender's hands, arms, or legs. Control of the assailant follows naturally thereon and enables the defender to subdue the assailant with a minimum expenditure of energy.

All of the considerations mentioned in connection with the use of the solo Lohan pattern apply equally well to the practice of the partner method of using the Lohan pattern, but, in addition, each training partner must have ample regard for the other's safety. Improperly executed technique, wrong acts at the wrong moments, badly focused punches, strikes, or kicks, and misused blocking or parrying actions can cause one or both training partners to be seriously injured. Always practice with safety in mind. Medicines should be applied after training if certain parts of the body have received enough shock to cause pain.

Alert trainees may notice what appear to be certain discrepancies between the performance of the solo Lohan pattern and the partner-practice method. Some portions of these two patterns do not fully agree with each other, but such differences are intended ones, and the trainee should not let them hinder his training.

APPLYING THE LOHAN PATTERN

Both the attacker and the defender execute mutual shaolin salutations (Fig. 1).

1. Applying the **Lohan Kai Kung** (page 84)

While the defender (left) is still in the salutation position, the attacker (right) quickly steps forward with his left foot and, using his right heel, delivers a front thrust-kick (*tern chiao*) to the defender's stomach (Figs. 2, 3). As the kick is released, the defender assumes the level-horse stance (*ping ma*) and blocks the kicking leg downward with the outer edge of his right forearm (Fig. 3). With his blocked kicking foot the attacker steps to the ground and immediately delivers a right thrust-punch (*chu ching*) to the defender's face (Figs. 4, 5). The defender quickly drops into a deep crouching posture, touching his right knee to the ground, and, with a sudden burst of speed and power, intercepts the punching arm with a blow from the knife-edge of his left hand, catching the punching arm at the wrist and pulling it upward over his head. The defender protects the front of his body with a covering action of his right arm and hand extended forcefully down the centerline in front of his body (Fig. 5).

2. Applying the **Chin Pu Chong Ch'uan** (page 86)

The defender rises and steps forward with his right foot and assumes a right triangle-horse stance (*san chiao ma*). At the same time, with a sudden burst of speed and power, he delivers a short right uppercut punch (*chong chui*), knuckles down, to the attacker's midsection just below his right ribs (liver area) (Fig. 6). The attacker, however, evades that punch by stepping back with his right leg and pulling his right arm free from the defender's grasp (Fig. 7).

3

8   9

3. Applying the **Sang Pu Swang Chuay** (page 87)

Assuming a left stance, the attacker positions both hands open, palms up, at his hips and comes forward one step with his right foot to deliver a double-hand knife-edge chopping-slicing action against the defender's ribs on each side of his body (Figs. 8, 9). The defender meets this attack by stepping forward with his left foot, spreading his arms high to his sides. Then, with a sudden burst of speed and power, he takes a short step forward with his right foot to bring that foot on line with his left foot. At the same time, he drives both arms, hands held as fists, forward and diagonally downward, inside the attacker's arms, wedge blocking the attacker's arms outward and then double punching (*cha chui*) both sides of the attacker's lower ribs with both fists, knuckles up (Figs. 9–12).

10

11

12

13

4. Applying the **Te Chiao Hern Tu** (page 88)

At the very instant of the defender's double punch (Fig. 13), the attacker evades the blows by quickly pivoting to his left and stepping back with his left leg, then immediately counterattacking with a roundhouse punch (*kwan arh ch'uan*) made with the top of his right fist and delivered to the left temple of the defender (Figs. 14, 15). (The movements in Figure 15 are not seen from the same angle as the movements in Figure 14. Angles shift to allow the greatest amount of detail to be seen as the exponents move and turn.) The defender turns to his left and, with a sudden burst of speed and power, assumes a left independent-leg stance (*han chi su*). At the same time, he blocks the attacker's punching right arm by using the hard top portion of his flexed left wrist and outer forearm in a split-block *tiau* fashion. The defender brings his right fist, knuckles down, to his right hip (Figs. 16, 17).

5. Applying the **Hey Hu Chuan Sing** (page 88)

Before the attacker can withdraw his blocked right arm, the defender steps forward with his left leg to a position outside the attacker's right leg, assumes a left triangle-horse stance (*san chiao ma*), and delivers a right forward thrust-punch (*chu ching*) to the attacker's right rib area. The defender protects his head by clenching his left fist and using the covering action of that arm (Figs. 18, 19).

116 · SHAOLIN: CHAPTER 4

14

15

16

17

5

18

19

6

20   21

6. Applying the **Lohan Yee Ting** (page 89)

The attacker avoids the defender's thrust-punch by
nimbly leaping to his left and assuming a left triangle-
horse stance (*san chiao ma*) (Figs. 20, 21, actions seen from
another angle). The attacker loses no time and launches
another attack, stepping forward with his right foot and
delivering a right thrust-punch (*chu ching*) to the defender's
exposed head (Figs. 22, 23). The defender avoids that blow
by weaving his upper body away from the punch; then,
with a sudden burst of speed and power, he turns to his
right to assume a right independent-leg stance (*han chi su*).
At the same time, he uses the knife-edge of his right hand in
a sweeping-block fashion against the outside of the attacker's
punching arm. The defender deflects the arm to his right
and covers it with the palm of the flexed wrist of his blocking right hand. The defender's left hand, wrist flexed, palm
open and down, covers his solar plexus (Figs. 24, 25).

22

23

24

25

7

7. Applying the **Yu Chuan Sing Tui** (page 90)

The defender keeps both hands open and wrists flexed and in the same relative positions as in the previous technique. He quickly raises his right leg, thigh parallel to the ground, and, with a sudden burst of speed and power, delivers a forward snap-kick (*chuan sing tui*) using the toes as a striking surface, to the heart region of the attacker (Figs. 26–28).

8. Applying the **Tui Pu Chey Chang** (page 90)

The attacker chops downward with his left bottom-fist to block the shinbone of the defender's kicking right leg, and knocks that leg down toward the ground. The defender steps to his right rear corner with his blocked right leg, but all the while maintains his relative arm and hand positions in order to protect his body (Figs. 29, 30). The attacker quickly continues his offensive. He slides his left foot up behind his right, shifts his weight onto that leg and delivers a roundhouse kick (*sau chiao*) against the defender's left rib area with the instep of the right foot used as a striking surface. The defender responds, shifting into a left independent-leg stance (*han chi su*). With a sudden burst of speed and power, he cuts forward and down with his open left hand, bringing that hand across the undersurface of his right arm and then using the knife-edge of the hand in a slicing-block (*che*) action directed down against the big muscles just above the knee of the attacker's kicking leg. The defender withdraws his right fist, knuckles down, to his right hip (Figs. 31, 32).

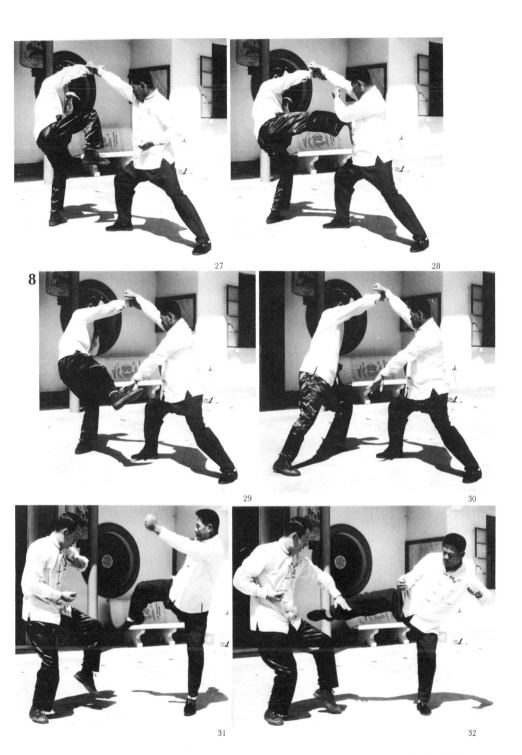

27

28

8

29

30

31

32

33   34

9. Applying the **Ching Kan Toh Yueh** (page 92)

The attacker steps to the ground behind himself with his blocked right leg and assumes a left stance, from which he instantly delivers a forward right thrust-punch (*chu ching*) aimed at the defender's chest. The defender steps backward with his advanced left leg, shifts his weight onto that leg, twists hard to his left, and sweeps his right arm circularly forward and inward in an outside block (*chiau*), using the outer edge of his right forearm and rotating his right fist so that the knuckles are forward and down as he blocks downward against the top of the attacker's forearm (Figs. 33, 34, actions viewed from another angle). The attacker continues his offensive by sliding his retreated right leg up behind his left leg, shifting his weight onto his right leg, and delivering a forward snap-kick (*liau ing tui*) against the defender's groin with his left leg, using the instep as a striking surface (Figs. 35, 36). The defender shifts, with a sudden burst of speed and power, into a right high independent-leg stance (*tu lie chiao*), using his raised right knee as a cover to protect his groin. At the same time, with his right bottom fist and the outer edge of that forearm, he cuts downward in scooping-block (*chiau*) fashion in toward his body to strike against the attacker's kicking right leg on the big muscles that lie just above the knee. The defender flings his left arm overhead, hand held as a fist, knuckles back (Fig. 36).

35

36

10

37

38

39

10. Applying the **Hern Ch'uan Chuan Sing** (page 92)

After having his kicking left leg blocked (Fig. 36), the attacker steps back and down with that leg, foot on line with his platform right leg. He shifts his weight onto the left leg and instantly steps forward a little with his right foot in an attempt to deliver a right-hand punch. The defender, however, moves with a sudden burst of speed and power and steps forward between the attacker's feet with his right foot to assume a right triangle-horse stance (*san chiao ma*). At the same time, he delivers a forward thrust-punch (*chu ching*) to the attacker's face with his right fist held vertically (Figs. 37–39).

FROM ANOTHER ANGLE: Figs. 43–44

11. Applying the **Lohan Chi Ku** (page 94)

In order to avoid the defender's punch, the attacker moves out of range by stepping back with his right leg (Fig. 40). He attempts to gain the initiative by sliding a bit forward while in a left stance, and then, from that stance, delivers a right thrust-punch aimed at the defender's face (Fig. 41, action viewed from a slightly different angle). The defender, in a right triangle-horse stance (*san chiao ma*), holds his ground and intercepts the punching arm from the inside by applying the outer edge of his left forearm against the inner surface of the attacker's arm and instantly catch-

42

43

ing that arm near the wrist to apply a sweeping block (*chiau*) with his left hand and pull the captured arm upward to his left (Figs. 41, 42). With a sudden burst of speed and power, the defender turns 180° to his left, pivoting on both feet in that direction. Simultaneously he continues to pull the captured right arm in the direction of his turn, and chops hard with the knife-edge (or bottom-fist) of his right hand against the base of the attacker's neck (Fig. 43). The attacker escapes the blow to his neck by leaping forward and turning around to his right to face the defender in a right stance (Fig. 44). The attacker then comes forward to

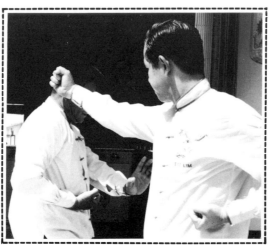

FROM ANOTHER ANGLE: Fig. 48

continue his offensive by aiming a right thrust-punch (*chu ching*) at the defender's chest (Fig. 45, action seen from another angle). The defender meets the attack by stepping forward with his right leg and blocks the oncoming blow by using the topside of his right forearm (that is, by rotating the knuckles of that fist downward) in an outside block (*chiau*) against the top of the attacking arm at the biceps (Figs. 46, 47). With a sudden burst of speed and power, the defender then assumes a right triangle-horse stance (*san chiao ma*) from which he delivers a short blow with his right back-fist to the right temple of the attacker (Fig. 48).

12

47

48

49

50

12. Applying the **Ching Kan Fu Hu** (page 96)

The attacker holds his ground but moves his head back out of range of the defender's blow, then quickly counter-punches with a right thrust-punch (*chu ching*) up under the defender's right arm and aimed at the defender's face. Standing in a right triangle-horse stance (*san chiao ma*), the defender blocks that punch from the inside with the outer edge of his left forearm, and instantly applies that hand in sweeping block (*chiau*) fashion to his left rear corner, catching the arm at the wrist (Fig. 49). The defender quickly grips the undersurface of the attacker's right arm near the armpit (triceps area) with his right hand, palm upward

51

52

(Fig. 50). With a sudden burst of speed and power, he
turns 180° to his left by pivoting on both feet in that direction and, using leverage applied with both of his arms
against the attacker's captured right arm, hurls the attacker
forward (Fig. 51). The attacker, in mid-flight, turns to his
left and comes onto the ground in a right stance facing the
defender. The defender assumes a left independent-leg
stance (*han chi su*) with his right fist raised above his head,
and his left fist positioned atop his left thigh (Fig. 52).

128 · SHAOLIN: CHAPTER 4

13

53

54

55

13. Applying the **Lohan Cho Hu** (page 96)

The attacker again quickly closes in on the defender, stepping forward with his left leg and delivering a right roundhouse kick (*sau chiao*) aimed at the defender's left rib area (Figs. 53, 54). The defender avoids that kick by stepping back with his left leg and, with a sudden burst of speed and power, assumes a right independent-leg stance (*han chi su*). At the same time he delivers a scooping block (*chiau*) with the outer edge of his right forearm and bottom-fist against the big muscles that lie just above the attacker's right knee. The defender uses his blocking arm to cut down and back in toward his body. He flings his left arm overhead (Figs. 54, 55).

56   57

60   61

14. Applying the **Swang Loong Chu Hai** (page 97)

Before the attacker can retract his blocked right leg, the defender jumps forward to assume a right triangle-horse stance (*san chiao ma*), and with a sudden burst of speed and power, delivers a double-punch (*cha chui*), his upper left fist, thumb down, to the right side of the attacker's head, and his lower right fist, thumb up, to the attacker's stomach (Figs. 56–58).

58   59

62   63

15. Applying the **Ting Su Yang Ch'uan** (page 98)

The attacker evades the defender's double punch by retreating, stepping back with his advanced right leg to assume a left stance (Figs. 59, 60). The attacker quickly slides forward in his left stance, and delivers a left thrust-punch (*chu ching*) aimed at the defender's head (Fig. 61). The defender responds by shifting his weight onto his rear left leg and assuming a right independent-leg stance (*han chi su*). Simultaneously, with a sudden burst of speed and power, the defender swings his right arm upward in front of his body to deliver an inside block (*ker*) made with the top of his right fist (that fist's knuckles rotated down) to the inner side of the attacker's left forearm (Figs. 62, 63).

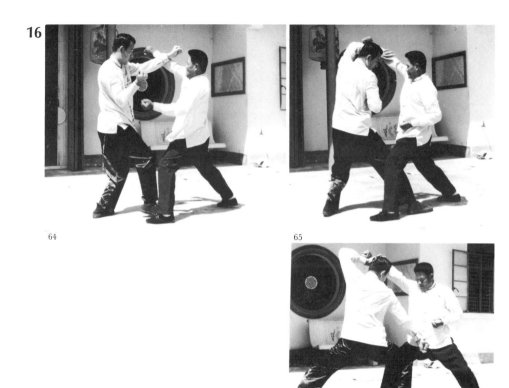

64

65

66

16. Applying the **Pai Yuen Ching Tao** (page 99)

His left thrust-punch blocked, the attacker aims a right thrust-punch (*chu ching*) at the defender's face. The attacker withdraws his left arm, fist to his left hip, to reinforce that blow (Fig. 64). The defender maintains his right independent-leg stance (*han chi su*) as he brings the outer edge of his left forearm against the inner surface of the attacker's punching right arm, and then executes a sweeping block (*chiau*) to grasp the attacker's arm with his left hand near the wrist. The defender pulls the captured arm over his left shoulder and upward to his rear (Figs. 64, 65). With a sudden burst of speed and power, the defender attempts to deliver a short inverted thrust-punch (*chung ing ch'uan*), thumb down, into the attacker's groin. The attacker avoids that blow by stepping to his rear with his advanced left leg. The defender is pulled into a right triangle-horse stance (*san chiao ma*) (Fig. 66).

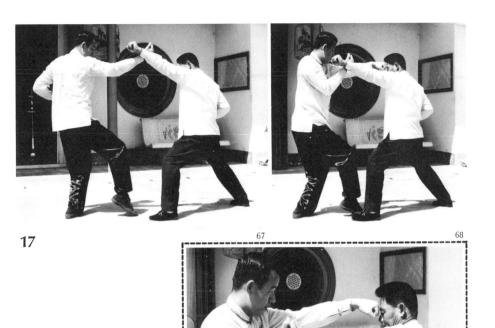

17

FROM ANOTHER ANGLE:
Fig. 68

17. Applying the **Erh Hu Chu Tung** (page 100)

The attacker assumes the initiative by stepping forward with his left leg and delivering a roundhouse punch (*kwan arh ch'uan*) with the top of his left fist to the defender's head, at the same time pulling his right arm free from the defender's grasp to position that fist at his right hip (Fig. 67, action seen from a different angle). The defender avoids that blow by shifting into a right independent-leg stance (*han chi su*), and blocking the attacker's blow with an inside block (*ker*) by rotating the fist knuckles down and using the inner edge of his right forearm against the inside surface of the attacker's left arm near the wrist. With a sudden burst of speed and power, the defender delivers a short punch (*twan ch'uan*) with his left fist, knuckles up, arm not fully extended, to the attacker's face. The defender's right arm, hand held as a fist, knuckles down, covers the attacker's left arm by pressing outward and downward against it (Figs. 67, 68).

18

69   70

18. Applying the **Tui Pu Ta Hu** (page 101)

The attacker holds his ground but moves his head back out of range of the defender's blow. Then, from his left stance at close range to the defender, he gives a forward left snap-kick (*liau ing tui*) to the defender's groin, using the instep as a striking surface. With the underside of his left arm, the defender presses the attacker's extended left arm down to break the timing of that kick. At the same time, the defender steps with his left leg around and behind his platform right leg to his right rear side, turning to his left to do so, and assuming a left triangle-horse stance (*san chiao ma*). With a sudden burst of speed and power, the defender blocks the kicking left leg from the outside using the top portion of his right forearm or (rotating his fist thumb down) his inverted back-fist, to knock the kicking leg inward across his body to his left (Figs. 69–71, actions viewed from a different angle). The force of the defender's blocking action turns the attacker around to his right and positions him with his back to the defender (Fig. 72).

19. Applying the **Fan Sao Chi Tui** (page 102)

Quickly the attacker turns to his right to face the defender in a right stance (Figs. 73–76). He then closes in on the defender once more, and aims a right-hand thrust-punch

71

72

19

73

74

75

76

(*chu ching*) at the defender's face (Fig. 77). The defender
attempts to assume a right independent-leg stance (*han chi
su*), but the attacker's offensive comes so quickly that the
defender is forced to meet that attack in a left triangle-
horse stance (*san chiao ma*). With a sudden burst of speed
and power, the defender twists his upper body to his left
and blocks the punching arm with an outside block of his
right forearm, bringing the outer portion of that arm hard
against the inside of the attacker's right forearm. The
defender blocks the attacking arm outward to his left (Figs.
78, 79).

20. Applying the **Ching Kan Tuan Chiu** (page 103)
   The defender steps quickly forward into a right triangle-
horse stance (*san chiao ma*), and delivers the point of his
elbow to the attacker's chest. The defender's left hand,
palm open and down, covers the attacker's right arm from
a position atop that wrist (Figs. 80, 81).

20

79

80

81

FROM ANOTHER ANGLE: Fig. 81

FROM ANOTHER ANGLE: Fig. 82

21. Applying the **Ching Kan Pu Min** (page 103)

With a sudden burst of speed and power, the defender delivers a right overhand arc-punch (*yang chiew*) made with his right back-fist to the nose of the attacker. The attacker moves out of range of that blow by stepping back with his advanced right foot and press blocking (*yah*) against the defender's right elbow with the palm of his left hand to slow the delivery of that arc-punch (Figs. 82–86).

22. Applying the **Chuan Sun Chiao Nan** (page 104)

The attacker instantly counterpunches with a right thrust-punch (*chu ching*) to the defender's face. The defender steps to his left with his left leg, and, with a sudden burst of speed and power, assumes a right level-horse stance (*ping ma*). At the same time, he twists his upper body to his right and delivers an outside block with the outer portion of his left forearm (rotating the knuckles of that fist downward) down against the biceps of the attacker's punching arm (Figs. 87–89, page 140).

21

82

83

84

85

86

22

87 88 89

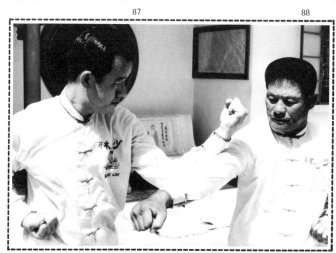

FROM ANOTHER ANGLE: Fig. 89

23. Applying the **Hey Hu Toh Sing** (page 104)

Standing with his feet in place in a left stance, the attacker throws a straight thrust-punch (*chu ching*) with his left fist to the face of the defender, who quickly moves his head back to his left and out of range of that blow. With a sudden burst of speed and power, the defender applies an outside block using the outer edge of his right forearm

140 · SHAOLIN: CHAPTER 4

23

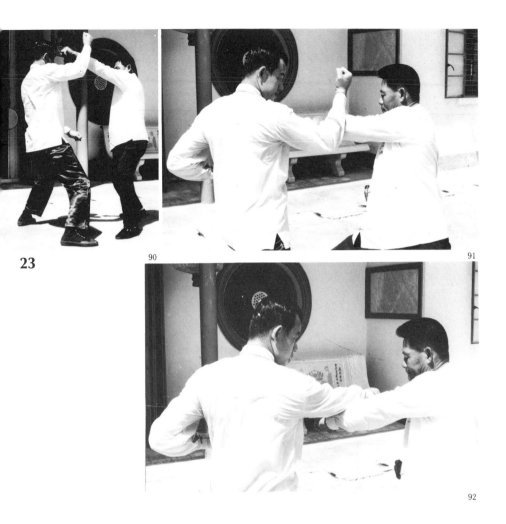

90

91

92

against the outside of the elbow of the attacker's punching left arm, twisting his upper body to his left to assume a level-horse stance (*ping ma*) (Fig. 90). Instantly, the defender drives his blocking right arm forward and down inside the attacker's left arm, forcing that arm down and outward as he delivers a short punch to the attacker's chest with his right fist. The defender brings his left fist, knuckles down, to his left hip (Figs. 91, 92).

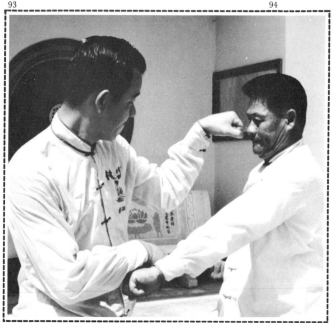

FROM ANOTHER
ANGLE: Fig. 93

24. Applying the **Ching Kan Chong Chui** (page 106)

Without a pause the defender twists hard to his right and, with a sudden burst of speed and power, withdraws his right fist to cover the attacker's left arm at the wrist. The defender deflects that arm outward and down as he delivers a short jab-punch (*twan ch'uan*) with his left fist, arm not fully extended, knuckles up (Fig. 93).

95

96

25. Applying the **Ching Kan Chiang Moh** (page 107)

The attacker weaves his upper body back out of range of the defender's short jab-punch, slides his left foot up close to his platform right leg, and, with the heel of his left foot, delivers a front thrust-kick (*tern chiao*) toward the groin of the defender (Figs. 94–96). The defender anticipates that kick. He steps backward onto his right leg and assumes a left high independent-leg stance (*tu lie chiao*). At the same time, with a sudden burst of speed and power, the defender applies a scooping block (*chiau*) with the outer edge of his left forearm or bottom-fist against the shinbone of the kicking leg, making a cutting motion downward and in toward his body with his blocking arm. He flings his right arm overhead (Fig. 96).

26. Applying the **Mung Hu Ju Tung** (page 109)

The attacker quickly retracts his blocked leg, placing that foot on the ground on line with his right foot, then, without a pause, shifts his weight onto his left leg and delivers a right roundhouse kick (*sau chiao*) aimed at the ribs of the defender. The defender steps back with his raised left leg and assumes a left triangle-horse stance (*san chiao ma*). He blocks down against the kicking leg with the outer edge of his right forearm against the shinbone of the kicking leg. He flings his left arm up overhead as his right fist covers his groin (Figs. 97, 98). The attacker steps to the ground with his blocked right leg and assumes a right stance (Figs. 99, 100).

99

100

103

27. Applying the **Lohan Sun Tien** (page 109)

The attacker presses in once more with a right thrust-punch (*chu ching*) aimed at the defender's throat (Figs. 101–103). The defender weaves his body back out of range of that punch, and then, with a sudden burst of speed and power, twists to his right and assumes a level-horse stance (*ping ma*). At the same time, he brings the outer portion of his right forearm against the attacker's punching arm from the outside in sweeping-block (*chiau*) fashion to grasp the

104

105

108

109

attacker's arm at the wrist (thumb down) (Figs. 104–106).
The defender then pulls that captured arm downward and
in toward his body, pinning it between his waist and his
right thigh as he steps forward with his left leg and delivers
an overhead downward blow with the outer edge of his left
forearm against the captured arm just above the elbow, at
the triceps area (Figs. 107–110). With his left arm, the
defender presses the attacker's arm down. The defender
releases his right-hand grasp of that arm to fling his own
right arm, hand held as a fist, knuckles back, overhead
(Fig. 111).

106

107

110

111

FROM ANOTHER ANGLE: Figs. 106–110

112   113

115   116

CLOSING THE PATTERN

Figures 112 to 118 show both training partners returning to an erect posture facing each other and mutually executing the shaolin salutation that closes this pattern.

114

117

118

Shaolin Training Methods

General

Shaolin, as an art, is a serious study. Those who regard shaolin as play are advised not to begin the study of this art. Shaolin involves the individual trainee in a very vigorous kind of physical effort and an unending process of mental discipline that should be followed throughout the course of the trainee's active life. Anyone who approaches shaolin training on a day-to-day basis, that is, expecting to see rapid and sensational results, is certainly headed for failure, and will probably lose all incentive for continuing training. Hard training over a protracted period of time is the key to success. Since the earliest days of this art there has been no general rule by which to predict when a trainee will reach levels of progress that will enable him to display an effective technique in a way that is satisfying to him.

Patience is perhaps the most important quality that must be developed by the trainee who engages in shaolin, for without this virtue little of lasting value can be achieved from training. In the process of developing a creditable technique, the trainee must repeat certain fundamental actions many times during each training session. This is laborious and boring, unless the trainee establishes the proper frame of mind. And, if the trainee expects that once these fundamentals have been mechanically mastered he will have an easier time of it as he participates in advanced training methods, he may be doomed to bitter disappointment when he is required by his instructor to apply these fundamentals in the form of prearranged pattern drills (*ii tao*) that must be repeated a countless number of times. The patterns mastered, the trainee must then learn the meaning of what he has up until now been practicing with blind acceptance and precision for several years. Finally, the trainee is faced with the most difficult of all tasks, the attainment of self-control. When he gains self-control, the trainee will never misuse his skill. This will signify mastery of both technique and himself and will be evidence of being fully trained in the art of shaolin.

Costume

Comfortable, loose-fitting garments of any type may be worn by a trainee who engages in shaolin, but the traditional costume shown in this book may be best. The outfit is made of a lightweight, durable kind of cloth (cotton or a synthetic fiber like rayon), and consists of a long-sleeved, high-collared, button-down-the-front kind of jacket and a pair of wide-cut trousers that fasten at the waist by means of a drawstring. According to the Hood Khar shaolin tradition, the jacket is light yellow and the trousers are black. No sash or belt is worn. The Chinese ideograms for the word *shaolin* and/or that word in English may be embroidered on the left side of the jacket at breast level. Most trainees also wear undergarments of some kind such as a tee-shirt and jockey or boxer-type shorts. An athletic supporter is optional.

Training Area

Shaolin training can be conducted in almost any area, either inside or out-of-doors. Traditional floor surfaces include those made of wood, stone, or cement. The training area should be of dimensions sufficient to provide a level surface for as many individuals as participate in training.

The training area should be well lighted. Good air circulation is essential.

Shaolin training requires a certain amount of equipment that is not particularly portable—sandbags, hardening stones, sand and pebble pits and pans—and thus a permanent training area at which this kind of equipment can be set up is the best kind of training facility.

Method

Begin your shaolin training with the practice of the

fundamentals described and illustrated in Chapter 2. Proceed slowly, in a step-by-step fashion, always respecting the recommended forms when you perform the various drills. Pay attention to the keypoints, which emphasize important elements in your performance. Bear in mind that speed of action will follow naturally on your ability to adhere to the proper form of what you are doing. Any half-way measures that you introduce into your practice will eventually prevent you from performing techniques effectively. Above all, you must follow the advice of your instructor. If you lack a competent instructor, a book like this one will aid you to some extent in your training, but it is doubtful whether you can achieve a high level of competency in shaolin through the use of a book alone.

Devote at least one hour of every training session to the practice of the fundamentals before attempting to perform the Lohan patterns shown in Chapters 3 and 4. Be sure that you are instantly able to assume each of the basic stances and postures: the level-horse stance (*ping ma*), the triangle-horse stance (*san chiao ma*), the independent-leg stance (*han chi su*), the high independent-leg stance (*tu lie chiao*), and the cat stance (*mao pu*). These are all precisely detailed in Chapter 2. As soon as you are reasonably familiar with the mechanics and forms of each of these basic stances and postures and you are able to hold yourself motionless in these stances for several minutes at a time, you should couple them with the basic punching and kicking exercises that are shown elsewhere in Chapter 2.

Anybody, even the least experienced novice, can assume a stance and make motions with his arms and legs as he attempts to punch and kick from that stance, but after a short period of time he begins to wobble, and his actions become feeble. Unless you are able to maintain the proper form of a stance throughout the time required to complete the recommended number of punches or kicks from that stance, the value of the drill will be lost. Therefore, strive to punch and kick from stable stances. Your inability to do that indicates that your body has not yet developed sufficient strength and flexibility for this vital task; greater effort must be given to training yourself in the form of the stances and postures.

It is not easy to punch and kick properly even from a stance that has been correctly assumed. However stable your stance may be, unless you learn to punch and kick with speed, accuracy, and effect, you are only making meaningless motions. Bring your hips into play as you punch and kick, as if making those actions from your midsection. This will help you to feel the movements that you are making. When making displacements, do so with speed and accuracy, stressing the coordination of your hands, wrists, forearms, eyes, upper body, legs, hips, and shoulders as you move. The basic punching, kicking, displacement, leg-strengthening, and hand-and-arm coordination drills that are shown in Chapter 2 are arranged in the accepted order of priority established by Hood Khar instructors. It is best to follow that recommended order, performing these drills each training session precisely as they are described. You may, however, rest a few minutes between the different drills. But the most dedicated of shaolin exponents make use of these short rest periods to toughen certain parts of their anatomy. Let us examine a few of the methods that they use for this purpose.

Hardening Your Anatomical Weapons

It is traditional for each shaolin exponent to devote a considerable portion of his training time to the use of special exercises that are designed to harden and make exceedingly durable certain portions of his anatomy. No matter what the exponent's degree of skill with technique, if he is to effectively apply his art in self-defense situations, he often will have to rely on the natural parts of his body as substitutes for weapons. This is especially the case when his assailant is also well trained in some art of combat. A fully trained shaolin exponent is capable of generating tremendous force when his fist, open hand, forearm, elbow, knee, or foot strikes a target. In order to protect himself from possible injury while practicing such strikes, the exponent must toughen his anatomical weapons. When the target is some vital part of an assailant's body, the shaolin exponent can easily inflict extensive damage on the assailant, even to the point of completely breaking the large bones of the latter's arms or legs with a single blow. Such drastic measures, however, are reluctantly taken by a shaolin exponent only if he fails to subdue an assailant by some less injurious means.

All the special exercises that are designed to toughen one's anatomical weapons must be used in compliance with a qualified instructor's advice; incorrectly applied, these methods can seriously cripple the exponent. After undergoing training to toughen his anatomical weapons, the trainee must also apply certain medicines to those areas. In addition, he may drink herbal teas. The medicines and teas offset the chances that there will be injurious effects from hard training, but such medicines and teas are compounded from secret formulae known only to qualified shaolin instructors. Thus, trainees are not advised to undertake any shaolin hardening methods without the guidance of an instructor.

TOUGHENING YOUR HANDS, FISTS, FOREARMS

Sand-Pan Method

This is a traditional shaolin method with which it is possible to develop the so-called shaolin iron palm (fist). Since this method is very unpleasant and destroys the nerves of the hands, it is not popular with modern exponents.

Sand is placed in a large, moderately deep, broad-rimmed iron frying pan and warmed over a fire. The pan is then set firmly on a solid base. The trainee who chooses to use this method does so on a daily basis for a period of from three to four months. Perform the exercise as follows:

1. Assume a level-horse stance (*ping ma*) close to the sand-filled iron pan (the thighs need not be held parallel to the ground).

2. Make a substantial number of actions with one hand at a time, such as thrusting the fingers of the hand into the sand, chopping the knife-edge of the hand down against the sand, punching the sand with different fist formations, or slapping the open palm or the back of the hand down onto the sand. You may use both hands in unison to dig into and lift sand in repetitive sifting actions with the palms or the backs of your hands.

3. As your hands become harder and tougher, increase the temperature of the sand you use. Also increase the coarseness of the sand, until finally you can use pebbles and small stones.

4. After training, apply medicine to the parts of your hands that have been thrust against the sand, pebbles, or stones.

Figures 1 to 8 illustrate these actions.

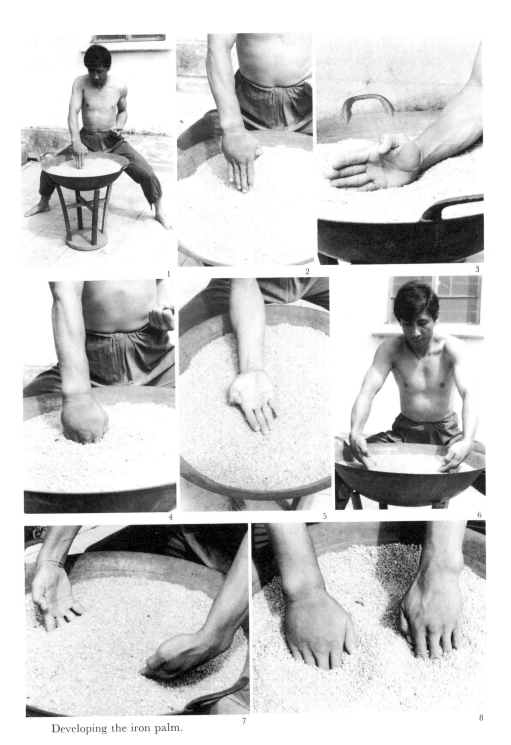

Developing the iron palm.

Stone-Block Method

Another of the traditional shaolin toughening methods used to train the hands, fists, and forearms makes use of a solid cylindrical block of granite or of some equally hard stone. This method is more popular with modern exponents of shaolin than the method just described; it is far less unpleasant than the pan method. The stone-block method, however, is a more gradual one, and it must be carried out for a long period of time, possibly several years.

The stone used in this method must be securely set atop some suitable base. Each time you train, toughen yourself as follows:

1. Assume any basic stance and deliver your hand, fist, or forearm in the manner of your choice (Figs. 1–7).
2. Use light tapping actions at first, gradually increasing the force of the actions as the parts of your anatomy that strike the stone become durable and tough. Force applied is more important than speed of delivery.
3. Strike the stone a substantial number of times with each part of your anatomy that you want to toughen in this manner.
4. Immediately after training, apply medicine to those parts of your body that have been exposed to the shock of impact against the stone.

Sandbag Method

Perhaps the most popular and most appropriate of shaolin toughening methods centers on the use of the sandbag. The hands, fists, forearms, elbows, and other parts of the body are quickly made durable by the use of the sandbag. The most important use of the sandbag in connection with this kind of shaolin training is that which leads to the development of the shaolin iron palm (fist). Hands and fists that have been trained in this manner become amazingly durable without a deadening of the nerves of the hands.

All sandbag training should follow several stages. In the first three of these stages you should assume a level-horse stance (*ping ma*) for the hand-hardening actions and a triangle-horse stance (*san chiao ma*) for those of the fist, forearm, and elbow. Use the sandbag toughening exercises at every training session, performing them in the following manner:

Developing the fist.

1

2

Developing the open hand.

4

5

Developing the forearm.

6

7

Stage 1 (first month): Slap, punch, or strike a ten-inch sandbag that has been filled with ordinary fine-grained sand. Do this 500 times slowly and lightly with each hand or arm. Apply medicine after each session.

Stage 2 (second month): Proceed exactly as you did in Stage 1, but use a fourteen-inch sandbag that has been filled with coarse-grained sand.

Stage 3 (third month): Proceed as you did in Stages 1 and 2, but use a sixteen-inch sandbag that has been filled with glass marbles.

Stage 4 (fourth month): Sit on the ground before a large, smooth-surfaced marble or granite slab and slap, punch, or strike it with various parts of your anatomy (hands, fists, forearms, elbows) 500 times. Immediately after training, apply medicine to the body parts toughened in this manner.

TOUGHENING YOUR FEET, KNEES, LEGS

Shinbones and Insteps

Exponents of shaolin concentrate on improving the durability of their legs so as to be able to absorb any shock directed against the shinbones and insteps. The simplest of the shaolin leg-toughening methods involves the use of a cylindrical piece of rattan cane about one-half inch in diameter. Tap this cane along your shinbone, from just below the knee to the ankle for ten to fifteen minutes during each training session. Apply medicine to the exposed parts on both legs immediately after such training. As your legs toughen and you grow able to withstand the force of such light blows without experiencing any pain, increase the force of the taps until you can take a hard blow. This achieved, substitute a flat piece of wood about one or two inches square for the cane, and proceed as before until both shinbones become numb each time you use this method. Continue using the piece of wood at each training session for four months. After that you should impact your shinbone against a heavy sandbag.

Concurrent with training to toughen your shinbones, it is also necessary to toughen your insteps. Using a frontal snap-kick action, strike the underside of a sandbag with your insteps, or use a roundhouse kick to strike the side of the bag with your insteps. Kick at least 100 times with each leg during every training session. The size of the sandbag used and the nature of its filling material should be varied in accordance with the three stages used in developing the hands and fists by the sandbag method. A wooden post that has been firmly set in the ground and wrapped with burlap or straw to provide a padded target is a good substitute for a sandbag. A fully trained exponent of shaolin is able to impact his insteps against an iron post that has been erected and padded in this fashion. When training to toughen the outer edges and the heels of your feet, impact these parts against a one-inch-thick wooden plank that has been set tightly up against a solid wall.

It is also necessary to develop and maintain the flexibility of your ankle joints as you toughen your feet. Do this through flexion exercises. Stand on one leg and raise the other leg, keeping it straight, until the toes are just off the ground. Point your toes downward. Flex the ankle so that you can point your toes up and back toward your shinbone; then point them down once again. Make clockwise and counterclockwise circles with your toes. Make ten flexing and ten circling actions with each foot. Do this every time you complete impact training for your insteps, and follow up with the application of medicine to the affected parts of your body.

Knees

The sandbag provides the best source of resistance when you train your knees to increase their durability and general toughness. Use the sandbag in exactly the same manner as you do when training your hands and fists. Never omit the use of medicine after training your knees.

MISCELLANEOUS TRAINING METHODS

Shoulders

Concentrate on making fast and powerful bumping actions with your shoulders against a sandbag or solid wall. Perform this action at least 100 times with each shoulder, doing so at five or six training sessions per month for a period of several years. Always use medicine on your shoulders after this toughening exercise.

Wrists

It is absolutely necessary that you strengthen your wrists

and improve their flexibility as you engage in shaolin training. One good method for doing so is to do the following:

1. Assume a triangle-horse stance (*san chiao ma*).
2. Hold a short length of stick, about two inches in diameter, in both hands.
3. Roll the stick around and around by twisting it with your hands, either in an alternating or cooperative way. Keep both elbows close to your body as you roll the stick.
4. Continue doing this until your hands cramp and become so tired that further training is impossible.
5. Apply medicine to the parts of your body affected by this training method.

Eyes

This traditional training method must be used with great care, and not without the understanding that it is possible to severely damage your sight through this method. But among the exponents of shaolin who have received traditional training, this method has proven to be reliable for achieving eye control. This exercise makes it possible to resist blinking even when certain actions are directed at one's face. Perform this exercise as follows:

1. Assume any basic stance as you stand before a lighted candle in a dark room.
2. Stare at the candle without blinking and slowly count to 100.
3. Close your eyes and concentrate on the rhythm of your breathing.
4. Go directly to sleep without opening your eyes.
5. On awakening, look first at the green foliage of a tree or bush so as to soothe the retinas of your eyes.
6. Apply medicine to your eyes to relieve the soreness that usually accompanies this kind of training.

少
林 **6**

Potpourri

Shaolin and Some Other Asian Combative Arts

A wide variety of different arts of hand-to-hand combat are found in Asia. Almost every Asian nation has its own systems of combat that are integral parts of its culture. The tremendous popularity of combative arts today is obvious; millions of advocates participate in and support the arts on a scale that has probably never before been matched.

It is an undeniable fact that Chinese shaolin and other Chinese arts of combat have strongly influenced the development of combative arts in other lands. For example, many of the present-day combative arts of Korea, Okinawa, and Japan have their prototypes in Chinese forms, although the former arts have taken on the special characteristics of the different ethnic groups supporting them and therefore deserve to be recognized as being distinctly different national arts of combat, non-Chinese in nature. In spite of the very strong influence of Chinese combative arts on those of Korea, Okinawa, and Japan, there are substantial technical differences in the make-up of the arts in these latter-named countries. In the earlier chapters of this book the characteristics of shaolin in general and the specific nature of shaolin of the Hood Khar pai in particular are discussed in some detail. The modern exponent of non-Chinese hand-to-hand arts such as Korean *T'ang su-do* and *taekwon-do,* and Okinawan and Japanese *karate-do* should, therefore, after reading this book and practicing the shaolin methods described herein, have firsthand experience with the many differences that exist between shaolin and the Korean, Okinawan, and Japanese arts.

But, to help the reader who cannot, for whatever reason, physically practice shaolin better understand these differences, a brief discussion follows.

Shaolin is considerably softer in nature than any of the Korean, Okinawan, and Japanese karate-like arts. This is largely so because of the circular pattern of the shaolin exponent's body movements when he applies his technique; the shaolin exponent first seeks to evade or blend with the forces of his adversary before retaliating in a hard and devastating fashion. Korean, Okinawan, and Japanese arts tend to be relatively more linear in matters of body displacement with the result being the tendency to meet resistance with resistance, that is, using a hard approach when dealing with an adversary. Then too, when advancing, the exponent of shaolin steps to the ground with his lead foot *heel first,* an action rarely utilized in Korean, Okinawan, or Japanese arts of combat. Shaolin, moreover, has a wider scope of techniques than any Korean, Okinawan, or Japanese combative art has. Each system of shaolin subsumes both sparring (boxing-like) and grappling (wrestling-like) categories of technique, with a substantial number of techniques making up each of these two categories. Korean, Okinawan, and Japanese karate-like arts, in particular, tend to minimize techniques of throwing and grappling on the ground, or to disregard them altogether; but such techniques are regular studies in shaolin.

Another salient difference between shaolin and the karate-like arts of Korea, Okinawa, and Japan is that in shaolin there is no emphasis placed on any kind of combative contact practice. There is no free-exercise kind of approach to the use of technique for the purposes of testing the relative skills of exponents, either in training or sporting competition. No really conclusive test is possible between exponents of shaolin except that which is made in a real fight, for shaolin techniques are inherently dangerous ones and do not easily lend themselves to control measures such as may be applied through expedients such as contest rules or the use of protective body armor. Shaolin, in its orthodox form, is not a game to be played for the entertainment of an audience or the whims of sports-minded exponents. Although there have been competitions between shaolin experts, none of these have proven satisfactory to orthodox practitioners of shaolin.

Finally, another clear example of the differences between

shaolin and the karate-like arts of Korea, Okinawa, and Japan is that shaolin makes judicious use of an extremely wide range of weapons. The karate-like arts of the Koreans, Okinawans, and the Japanese tend to play down the use of weapons.

Weapons of Shaolin

Genuine shaolin systems and highly trained shaolin exponents are recognized by the fact that weapons are not alien to them. It is outside the limits of this introductory book to list all of the weapons that are used by shaolin experts. These instruments are numerous and vary as to types among the different pai, but some commonly used types among shaolin experts can be mentioned. These are the straight double-cutting-edged sword (*chien*), the curved single-cutting-edged sword (*tau*), the tufted single-bladed spear (*ch'iang*), the long staff with either a unidimensional or single-taper cross-section (*koon*), and the short-hafted heavy halberd (*kwanto*). Hood Khar experts also include among their favorite special weapons the ringed metal-headed monk's staff (*chan-chang*) and the straight iron-bar truncheon (*kan*).

Many of these shaolin instruments are designed to be weapons, but there is also a rather large number of tools and objects of domestic use that serve the shaolin exponent as weapons. These common instruments include hoes, rakes, baskets, umbrellas, and benches. The shaolin exponent can thus be said never to be unarmed; he is trained to pick up any object and to use it effectively as a weapon.

Weapons training is a regular part of the shaolin training regimen, but only after a reasonable degree of skill has first been attained by the exponent in the use of fundamentals found in this book does he normally train himself with weapons. Weapons training methods and techniques are beyond the scope of this book.

Glossary-Index

neow poh. See mao pu
Northern Shaolin, 20–21
Northern Wei dynasty, 13

open-hand and arm use, 68–79

pah poh kang. See pai pu kung
pai (generic name for an organization devoted to the study of Chinese combative arts), 20
pai her liang tsu ("white crane" training exercise), 71–73
pai pu kung ("100-steps" training exercise), 60–62
Pai Yuen Ching Tao (16th Lohan sequence: "White Monkey Plucks Fruit"), 99, 132
pa-kua (a Chinese hand-to-hand art within the so-called internal systems), 18
peh-beh. See ping ma
pei hok kwi sit. See pai her liang tsu
ping chui (forward double-punch consisting of a straight thrust-punch and an overhead arc-punch made at the same instant), 97
ping ma (level-horse stance), 27–28, 84, 104, 106, 109, 138, 141, 145
pok tui. See fu tui
posture, 26–40
Pratyeka-Buddha, 81
prearranged exercises. See ii tao
punches: double fist (see cha-chui); forward double (see ping chui); overhand arc (see yang chiew); round-house with top-fist (see kwan arh ch'uan); short inverted thrust (see chung ing ch'uan); short jab (see twan ch'uan); short uppercut (see chong chui); thrust, to the front (see chu ching)
P'u-t'i-ta-mo. See Ta Mo

sakah-beh. See san chiao ma
san chiao ma (triangle-horse stance), 30, 86, 88, 92, 94, 97, 99, 102, 103, 109, 112, 116, 118, 123, 124, 126, 127, 130, 132, 134, 136, 144
Sang Pu Swang Chuay (3rd Lohan sequence: "Double Step and Double Punch"), 87, 114
sau chiao (roundhouse, hook, sweep, and sickle kicks), 55, 120, 129, 144
secret societies, 16
shaolin (generic name for a category of Chinese combative art), 9, 10, 15, 16, 18, 20, 21, 81, 163; area for training, 151; costume, 151; etiquette, 22–26, 84, 109, 112, 148; history, 15–17; legend, 13–15; medicine, 154–60; training equipment, 154–63; training methods, 150–60; weapons, 163
Shaolin Temple, 13, 14, 15, 16, 17, 20
Shih-pa Lohan Shou ("Lohan eighteen hands," series of basic exercises believed to be the original basis of shaolin), 82
short-punching, 50–52
siah mien ch'uan (bottom-fist), 41, 92
Six Supernatural Powers, 82
Southern Shaolin, 20–21
stances, 26–40; cat (see mao pu); high independent-leg (see tu lie chiao); independ-

ent leg (see *han chi su*); level horse (see *ping ma*); triangle horse (see *san chiao ma*)

Sung dynasty, 18

Sung Shan, 13

Swang Loong Chu Hai (14th Lohan sequence: "Double Dragon Goes Out to Sea"), 96, 130

taekwon-do, 161

Ta-hung Men (a main branch of Southern Shaolin), 20

t'ai chi ch'uan (a Chinese hand-to-hand art within the so-called internal systems), 18

Ta Mo, 13, 15, 16

T'ang su-do, 161

T'an Tsung, 14

Ta-sheng Men (shaolin system based on the antics of the monkey), 20

Ta Tsun-shen, 14

tau (curved single-cutting-edged sword), 163

Te Chiao Hern Tu (4th Lohan sequence: "Iron Bridge Across a Stream"), 88, 116

teh keng (short-punching actions), 43, 50–52

tern chiao (front thrust-kick), 54, 56–58, 112, 143

Three Insights, 82

tiau (rising split block), 68, 88

ting sik. See *han chi su*

ting su. See *han chi su*

Ting Su Yang Ch'uan (15th Lohan sequence: "Instant Block and Strike"), 98, 131

tok lip kah. See *tu lie chiao*

toughening the anatomy: feet, knees, legs, 158–59; hands, fists, forearms, 154–58; shoulders, 159; wrists, 160

training methods: sandbag, 156–58, 159; sand-pan, 154; stone-block, 156

triangle-horse stance. See *san chiao ma*

Ts'ai-chia Ch'uan (a main branch of Southern Shaolin), 20

Tui Pu Chey Chang (8th Lohan sequence: "Step and Slice"), 90–91, 120

Tui Pu Ta Hu (18th Lohan sequence: "Retreat and Strike the Tiger"), 101–2, 134

tu lie chiao (high independent-leg stance), 36–37, 90, 92, 100, 122, 143

tung keng (long-punching actions), 43, 44–49

twan ch'uan (short jab-punch made with knuckles up), 100, 106, 133, 142

wai chia (external systems of Chinese combative arts), 18

weapons of shaolin, 163

Wei-t'o Men (shaolin system based on the virtues of deities), 20

"white crane" exercise. See *pai her liang tsu*

wu kung (generic term for skillfully executed combative action), 18

wu shu (generic name for Chinese martial arts), 17–18

yah (downward block using the top of the forearm), 70, 138

yang chiew (overhand arc-punch), 94, 98, 102, 103, 138

Yin Hung-shen, 16

Yu Chuan Sing Tui (7th Lohan sequence: "Kick To Pierce the Heart"), 90, 120

Yue (a main branch of Northern Shaolin), 20